SPC FOR PRACTITIONERS:

Special Cases and Continuous Processes

SPC FOR PRACTITIONERS:

Special Cases and Continuous Processes

Gary Fellers

SPC FOR PRACTITIONERS:
Special Cases and Continuous Processes

Gary Fellers

Library of Congress Cataloging-in-Publication Data

    Fellers, Gary.

    SPC for practioners : special cases and continuous

    processes / by Gary Fellers.

    p. cm.

    Includes bibliographical references.

1. Process control — Statistical methods. I. Title.

TS156.8F45   1991

658.5'62'015195—dc20   91–6454

                                  CIP

ASQC Quality Press, American Society for Quality Control
310 West Wisconsin Avenue, Milwaukee, Wisconsin 53203

ISBN 0-87389-102-3

10987654321

Acquisitions Editor: Jeanine L. Lau

Production Editor: Tammy Griffin

Printed in the United States of America

TABLE OF CONTENTS

PREFACE

This book contains a user's guide to statistical process control (SPC) charts. The concept of chance variability and the SPC rationale are explained. The application of SPC procedures to discrete, continuous, and batch-type processes is explained. These applications include charts for X-bar ($\bar{x}$), range, percent nonconforming, number of nonconformities, demerits, and individuals. The use of these tools is illustrated with actual case studies and some common pitfalls are described. A discussion on the concept of process capability is included. Several frequently occurring special cases of processes are discussed. There are brief sections on SPC for administrative variables and problem-solving techniques. There are introductory sections that should make this book suffice for all practitioners. All SPC special-case issues are not included, only those relating to questions posed by the author's consulting clients from several hundred processes over the last decade. Apparently most other issues are well-discussed in the literature since the author's clients have been able to apply them with no help from him. Novices may want to read section 2.1 before beginning this book. This section will enable the reader to understand the classic formulas, which do not apply for many special-case processes.

ACKNOWLEDGMENTS

The author would like to thank ASM International (Metals Park, OH 44073) for their permission to use the artwork from their videocourse entitled, "Solving Problems with Statistical Process Control." The clerical accuracy for this book must be attributed to Sharon B. Young, who did all the hard work. The conceptual correctness must be dedicated to my wife Pam Fellers, who keeps my mind clear. My parents, Jackie and George Fellers, gave me the motivation to begin learning at an early age. The testers from industry were:

Mr. Larry W. Baird, Augusta Newsprint

Mr. Allen Evans, NUS Corporation

Mr. Barry Norton, DSM Chemicals

Mr. James Tadlock, Weyerhaeuser

Dr. Nabil Ibrahim, Augusta College

CHAPTER 1
What SPC Is
and
What It Does

Introduction and Implementation Guidelines

There is an old expression among quality control professionals that goes something like: "You cannot efficiently inspect quality into a product after it has left the process. Quality must be manufactured into the product during the production process."

From a layman's point-of-view, statistical process control (SPC) is the practice of this truism. The basic steps in establishing an SPC program follow:

- The producer identifies the in-process characteristics of the product that affect fitness for use.

- An in-process sampling plan is designed to measure or observe the selected characteristics.

- These measurements are plotted on a control chart.

- Corrective action is taken whenever the charts indicate that a significant change in the process has taken place.

The above systematic evaluation enables the producer to identify problems in their early stages, perhaps before any nonconforming product is manufactured. The use of statistical guidelines enables the producer to decide whether a process adjustment should be made. This eliminates the temptation to overcontrol the process (make too many adjustments), or to undercontrol the process (make too few adjustments). Overcontrol and undercontrol will decrease product quality. It is most effective to begin SPC as far upstream in the process as possible, unless customer pressure or politics dictate otherwise. Also, it is a must to implement SPC on a project-by-project basis. Concentrate on one or two variables at a time in the same department. The technical staff must thoroughly experiment with the total procedure before the tailor-made training program is created to train the operators. Train operators and supervisors the day before SPC begins in their department, not in large groups weeks before they will use the training. Prior to training the operators, all levels of plant management must have two to three hours of visionary training. This involves the who, what, when, why, how, etc., of SPC implementation. Generally it is preferable to let an experienced SPC professional (usually a consultant) perform this upper management training with company data and examples. At the outset, SPC implementation may impart mass confusion, especially if too many projects or departments are begun too soon. This is especially true if the SPC coordinator is inexperienced. The benefits of SPC take three to six months to begin to surface. Therefore, it must be explained to upper management that because results are not always immediate and SPC implementation may be confusing at first, they must be somewhat autocratic at the outset. It should be stated at the beginning to all levels of management that SPC is *going* to happen, and that the SPC coordinator is going to help to train them on a project-by-project basis. In three to six months, if properly implemented, SPC will catch-on with no further force by upper management.

There are always several perennial problems on every process, such as uncalibrated instruments or sensitivity problems with control mechanisms. Even though it is not the case, in the minds of the operators, SPC is not feasible (or useful) until these things are fixed. The best way to start SPC off on the right foot is for the SPC coordinator to uncover a few of these issues and to follow through with management to get these things repaired. Then the operators are ready to do their part.

Upper management always asks questions about the traits needed by the SPC coordinator. To begin with, the coordinator should never be the person who doesn't seem to fit in anywhere else. If it is not an obvious sacrifice to release the person for one to two years to be the SPC guru, the wrong person has been chosen. From a technical perspective, the SPC coordinator needs several years experience in this industry, and preferably a technical degree. An extra five years of experience as well as superb communicative skills can be more important than a degree. From a personal perspective, the most important traits are:

1. Communicates extremely well.

2. Can tolerate ambiguity.

3. Fits in with hourly operators.

4. Likes to experiment.

5. Is patient.

6. Can use a PC, etc.

As you can see, the SPC candidates are in short supply. You are doomed to fail, however, without a good one!

1.1
Concept of Chance Variation (Random Variation)

A perfectly controlled process will yield product whose characteristics still vary. It is impossible to exactly duplicate an item no matter how stringent the controls. This deviation, which is inherent in the process, is said to be the random process variability (also known as common cause by many practitioners). Figure 1.1 shows a tally of the weight of a manufactured product from a typically controlled process. The variability in weight is caused by the inherent randomness of the process (common cause).

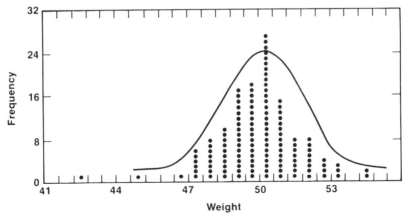

Figure 1.1 Concept of Chance Variability

To understand the process that generated the tally of Figure 1.1, suppose that during a period when the process was stable (no changes occurred in the manufacturing processes), 100 bags, whose fill weight was nominally 50 pounds, were weighed. As one can see, not all bags weigh exactly 50 pounds. Most weights are close to 50 pounds and the probability of obtaining bag weights greatly different than 50 pounds decreases rapidly. It would be unusual to have six or seven successive bags weigh more than 51 pounds. We expect, however, an occasional bag to weigh 51 or more pounds. All industrial processes have some random variation similar to this bagging example. We often say that this variability is *common to the system.*

The spread of values in the tally of Figure 1.1 mostly represents the chance variability for this process that is common to the system and cannot be removed in the short-term. The goal of SPC is to stabilize the process such that the average is at a specified level, often at the nominal specification value, and to ensure that the remaining process variability is only common cause. In statistical terms, the peak of the tally, or average, should be on the desired target value and the spread of values about the target should be at the minimum for the process.

The initial step in any SPC study is to sample the process in order to obtain an estimate of the process variability. A simplified procedure for accomplishing this will be outlined at the beginning of Chapter 2. If many samples were drawn from the process, measured, and the resulting histogram plotted using small cell boundaries, the result would be a smooth curve which represents the distribution of the possible measurements from the process. The bell-shaped curve of Figure 1.1 represents an estimate of the theoretical distribution. Statisticians often call this theoretical entity the *probability distribution of the measurements*. Most practitioners call it the bell curve.

Although the tally in Figure 1.1 is sometimes useful in industrial applications, other types of charts, as in Figure 1.2, are more frequently used in conjunction with SPC. These charting procedures assist the manufacturer in centering the process on target and controlling process variability. There are several techniques outlined in this book to accomplish this goal.

In a typical application for controlling the process average and variability of our bag weight example, a sample of five consecutive bags would be selected periodically from the process. The average and range of the sample of the five bags are then calculated. If the average is within the statistical limits of the chart, the process is temporarily considered to be on target. If the range is below the upper limit, the process variability is temporarily considered not to have increased.

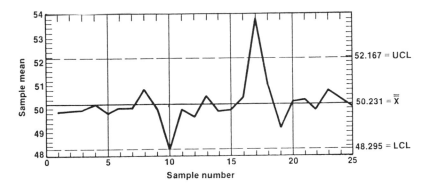

Figure 1.2 Typical Control Chart

The control chart for the process average is shown in Figure 1.2. (The symbols on the chart are explained later in Section 1.4.) Note that the average for sample number 17 is above the upper control limit (UCL). This indicates that the process needed adjustment at that point. Samples one through 16 do not indicate any change in the process level and are within the limits of the expected chance variability. These limits are called the control limits. (Explicit control chart procedures are outlined in Section 2.1.)

1.2
Example of Overcontrol

As an example of overcontrol, consider the case where an operator weighs one randomly selected heavy bag of 51 pounds from the distribution of Figure 1.1. With no understanding of statistical control limits, the operator may adjust the process downward. Then, after the next sampling, he or she would likely adjust the process upward. As shown in Figure 1.3, this constant tampering may substantially increase the product variability since the process average is shifted each time an adjustment is made. There are many cases of overcontrol where the producer caused the total product variability to increase by more than 25 percent by adjusting the process when management had not established statistical limits and control criteria for the operators. (Note who is designated as having the responsibility of giving the operators a "road map.")

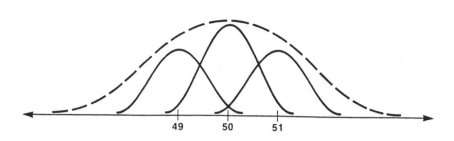

Figure 1.3 Example of Tampering

Pertaining to histograms taking accumulated daily or weekly averages of the batches represented in Figure 1.3 may indicate that the process average is acceptable. A control chart, however, would probably show the process average to have shifted several times. The customer likely buys and uses single bags, one at a time, not as a group. The long-term average is not as important as the short-term variability in most cases. The overcontrol has caused the unit-to-unit variability to be considerably greater than was necessary. On a first visit to a plant that is overcontrolling, the plant manager typically will indicate that, "One minute we have to turn it down; then the next minute we have to turn it up again!" Apparently, they are not aware of the problems caused by overcontrolling. There are numerous cases where a process was in a good *state of statistical control,* which meant that Figure 1.1 could have applied, however the operators of the process were instructed to overreact and to make unnecessary process adjustments approximately every hour. Yet, once SPC was installed, the operators found adjustments seldom were necessary.

1.3
Undercontrol

A process will eventually drift to yield results that appear the same as those in Figure 1.3. In these cases, failure to react is called *undercontrol*. When there are reasons behind measured process variability, assignable cause is said to exist. Assignable causes frequently are referred to as local (special) faults, since the problem most likely is local to the immediate process, and not common to the system. A good SPC charting procedure will enable the operator to recognize when assignable cause (or local faults) exists. However, variability common to the system usually can be addressed effectively only with the help of upper management. Assignable causes of variability have reasons behind them; however, there is always some level of chance variability that cannot be readily eliminated. The procedures in this book will help you methodically establish the natural capability limits for a process which represent the chance variability. The procedure is simple, but must be followed precisely and subjected to experimentation before presentation to the operators.

1.4
Control Limits versus Specification Limits

In Figure 1.4 a case is shown where the customer's specification limits are within the natural tolerances of the process. The upper and lower specification limits are identified as USL and LSL, respectively. The process upper and lower natural (control) limits are identified as UCL and LCL. (These are control limits for individual measurements, not averages. The reason for this statement will be obvious later.)

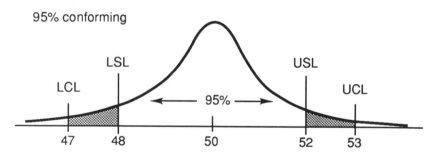

Figure 1.4 Specification Limits Within Control Limits

Pressure on the operators to do better will not solve the problem of Figure 1.4 where a properly centered process will still produce some out-of-specification product. The production operators probably will be alienated because management has failed to accept one of the inevitable alternatives (listed below) for cases where the process is incapable of staying within the customer specifications. These alternatives are:

1. Inspect each item of output to screen out the defectives (if feasible).

2. Redesign the process to reduce its natural variability. This alternative typically involves a large investment in engineering and capital expenditures. The team approach explained in Section 5.1 is usually required to permanently reduce the common cause.

3. Use SPC in the meantime to keep the process on target and prevent the shaded areas under the curve from becoming even larger. In the long run, items 1 or 2 will be necessary, unless the customer relaxes his product requirements. Then an inexpensive SPC program will enable the operators to keep the process on target.

1.5
Controlling to Capability Limits versus Specifications

The major thrust behind SPC is that the process must be controlled based on its inherent capabilities. Controlling to the customer's specifications, or any other set of limits, will cause an increased level of defectives. We may inspect and sort based on specifications, but we make process adjustments based on control charts. Also, controlling to customer specification limits that are wider than the process, inherent capability limits causes the customer to receive more product considerably off-target than he or she would if SPC were being used. This concept is demonstrated in Figure 1.5.

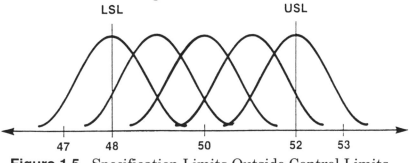

Figure 1.5 Specification Limits Outside Control Limits

In today's marketplace, customers are pressuring vendors to use SPC and to engineer their processes to have capability indexes (to be defined later) greater than 1.0 units. This implies that the entire specification range is not to be used. In the long run, this is the only cost-effective procedure. There are many purchase orders stating not only that the product be within specification, but that the vendor must demonstrate that the process is in statistical control. Demonstration of the use of an effective SPC program is the only method of meeting this requirement. Competition from top-quality foreign and domestic producers has caused customers to begin to request this increased level of quality.

1.6
Overview of Three Basic Categories of Processes and Control Charts

This book contains discussions about the three major categories of industrial processes. The first to be discussed is the process that produces discrete units of product, such as machined parts. In these cases each item is produced individually such that all sources of inherent random variability have an opportunity to occur between successive units of manufactured items. In these cases, the within-subgroup ranges probably provide an accurate representation of the total process common cause. These are the simple cases covered by most SPC textbooks. Discrete processes are presented here only as a contrast to continuous processes. The thrust of this book is special cases, particularly continuous processes.

When the relevant product characteristics are measurable, such as widths, weights, tensile strengths, etc., the recorded information is called *variables data*. The $\bar{x}$ chart and the range chart often apply in these cases. (Chapter 2 contains a discussion of these control charts.) Occasionally, the control chart for individuals of Section

2.9 will apply for discrete processes when sampling is extremely expensive and the short-term, plus-or-minus variability away from the process centering is reasonably small and stable. When calculations on the shop floor are not feasible, the median charts on page 140 may be employed.

Many processes, such as paper-making machines, extruders, or chemical plants, are continuous and do not produce discrete items of product. Any subgrouping for packaging or sampling purposes will be for customer or producer convenience and will not likely form a rational subgroup for statistical computing purposes. If $\bar{x}$ charts are constructed in the classical fashion for continuous processes, the calculated control limits typically will be from 10 to 50 percent too close to the process target and impossible to stay within. The control charts for individuals of Section 2.9, or some close adaptation of this technique, apply in these cases. Control charts for individuals also apply to most types of accounting data. Several practical examples of continuous processes are presented in Chapter 2.

Batch processes also are discussed in Chapter 2. Fundamental statistical concepts will be used to establish control limits and sampling plans for these types of processes. With batch processes, it is necessary to distinguish between within-batch and between-batch sources of chance variability.

Quality characteristics that cannot be measured, but must be classified or counted, are called *attributes*. An example would be the many pass-fail quality attributes.

Control charts for attributes will be discussed in Chapter 3. These attribute charts include p charts, c charts, np charts, u-charts, and demerit per unit charts. Demerit control charts are becoming more popular in cases where there are many attributes to be observed and the various characteristics are of differing importance. A control chart for demerits can help the manager determine if the overall quality system is operating. These demerit charts have been applied to many types of product such as magazine print quality or CRT output quality. An example is discussed in Section 3.5 pertaining to a demerit chart kept in a magazine printing plant. The control charts for attributes of Chapter 3 are a last resort when a variables chart cannot be used.

Chapters 4 and 5 contain some comments pertaining to the management of an SPC program and problem solving. Training requirements will be specifically outlined in Chapter 5. Many firms undertrain the operators while attempting to overtrain them. (We all cannot be theoretical statisticians.) Section 5.1 contains some guidelines pertaining to problem solving. Many manufacturing facilities have matured to the point that most of the obvious problems that can be singularly solved by one person have been eliminated. The remaining problems likely will necessitate a think tank team drawing on many departments using some of the formalized approaches in Section 5.1. This is especially true when trying to reduce the level of common cause.

For each of the control chart chapters, several factors will be addressed:

1. The sample (subgroup) size to be used. (Five specimens is not always a requirement.)

2. The sampling frequency.

3. Which statistical formulas are to be used.

4. The sampling plan or subgrouping method to be employed.

Often items 1 through 3 are straightforward. Item 4 may be somewhat complicated, especially for continuous processes.

From a theoretical point of view, SPC is always the best technique for economically producing a quality product. In the short-term, however, SPC may be of limited value for any of the following cases. (1) Some operations are in such a poor state of statistical control that the process average shifts too frequently for any type of feasible SPC sampling interval to be employed. (2) Movement similar to that of Figure 1.3 may occur rapidly. (3) The width of the process distribution or level of random variation may change frequently over time.

The best way to identify extremely unstable processes is to precisely follow the SPC rules while sampling as frequently as temporarily feasible. Then, if assignable cause occurs more often than every eight or so plottings on the control chart, the process must be repaired, or redesigned before proceeding with an SPC program. The only other option is to screen all the output.

Plotting measurements from all units of output prior to trying SPC is always a recommended procedure. An analysis of this plot may indicate that the process distribution is shifting or changing shape too frequently for any feasible sampling plan to work. Section 5.1 contains an overview of problem solving that may be helpful in such cases.

In any case, the long-term job of any SPC practitioner is to track down and eliminate all variability through detailed process analysis and problem solving. Twenty to 80 percent of what appears to be common cause at the outset can be identified as assignable cause with the appropriate problem-solving tools, through an interdisciplinary team. This takes many months, and sometimes years, but the payoff always is tremendous. SPC also may be difficult to implement when production runs are short. If enough points cannot be plotted in time to react, and thus to improve the rest of the lot, some kind of statistical lot acceptance plan may be as good as SPC. (See Section 2.10 for an alternative for small lot sizes.) In any event, if there is a quality problem, the prevention mode of Section 5.1 is necessary for short production runs.

Prior to trying SPC many managers believe that all their processes are like the ones described in the previous paragraph. In most cases, however, they have mistaken random variation (common cause) as local faults (assignable cause). Giving SPC a chance typically solves many of their quality problems. Experience shows that the plus-or-minus process limits usually are reduced approximately 25 percent when SPC is implemented.

CHAPTER 2
Control Charts for Averages
(X-bar Charts)

This chapter contains a discussion of $\bar{x}$ control charts for averages. These are the most common types of control charts. The $\bar{x}$ charts, as defined here, only apply for processes that produce discrete items such as nuts, bolts, axles, etc. There must be ample opportunity for process chance variability to manifest itself between consecutive units of product for $\bar{x}$ charts to be used. When this is the case, the within subgroup ranges provide an accurate representation of total process common cause. Chemical plants, paper-making machines, extruders, etc., typically cannot be controlled with $\bar{x}$ charts when using the average-range technique. The customary $\bar{x}$ charts, with limits based on the average ranges within small groups of product consecutively sampled, usually will have control limits that are too tight for such continuous processes.

Several examples will be provided in later sections for continuous, batch, and discrete processes, but first let's discuss a case study where $\bar{x}$ charts apply.

2.1
Bag Weight Example of X-bar Control Charts

A ceramics firm is mixing a powdered material in a batch operation. Let's assume that a single mixed batch supplies the bagging process for four hours. The customer wants 50-pound bags, yet it is too costly to weigh each bag as part of the process. The process blows material into the bags for a preset time period which is based on a potentiometer setting. Every 30 minutes the operator samples five consecutive bags, weighs them, and calculates the average and the range of the five to determine if the potentiometer needs adjusting. The data, the averages, and the ranges, are shown in Table 2.1 on page 25. The average and the range of the first subgroup are calculated as follows:

$$\bar{x} = \frac{49.1 + 50.0 + 48.8 + 50.5 + 51.0}{5} = 49.9 \qquad (1)$$

$$R = 51.0 - 48.8 = 2.2 \qquad (2)$$

An x̄ chart applies here since the quantity of material blown into consecutive bags was done in a distinctly independent fashion. If one bag is randomly heavy, there probably is no reason to expect the next bag to be heavy also. However, if instead of bag weight the product characteristic was fractional composition of the batch constituents, one would not use standard x̄ charts with this sampling method. Since a batch lasts four hours, any subgroup within this interval likely will consist of specimens that are very similar, especially if the batch is mixed properly. Any within-subgroup variability for composition will represent mostly measurement system deviations, not the process blowing operation common cause variability. We will return to this example later.

The individual datum points are plotted in Figure 2.1.

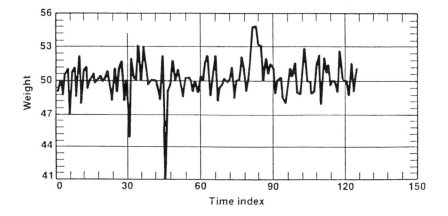

Figure 2.1 Individual Bag Weight Plot

Table 2.1 Bag Weight Data

Subgroup	Subgroup Data					$\bar{x}$	R
1	49.1	50.0	48.8	50.5	51.0	49.9	2.2
2	47.2	50.7	51.1	48.6	52.1	49.9	4.9
3	48.1	51.0	51.2	49.4	50.1	50.0	3.1
4	50.5	49.9	50.1	50.3	50.0	50.2	0.6
5	50.1	50.7	49.4	48.2	51.1	49.9	2.9
6	49.1	51.1	51.6	48.3	50.1	50.0	3.3
7	45.0	51.9	50.2	50.1	53.1	50.1	8.1
8	50.1	52.9	51.5	49.7	50.0	50.8	3.2
9	50.1	50.1	49.6	48.3	52.1	50.0	3.8
10	41.2	49.1	49.4	51.7	50.1	48.3	10.5
11	51.0	49.8	48.7	50.2	50.2	50.0	2.3
12	50.0	49.1	49.9	49.1	50.3	49.7	1.2
13	50.0	51.6	52.2	48.8	50.1	50.5	3.4
14	52.1	48.2	49.4	49.7	50.2	49.9	3.9
15	49.9	50.1	51.2	48.5	50.1	50.0	2.7
16	50.1	52.1	51.1	49.2	50.1	50.5	2.9
17	53.2	54.7	54.8	53.3	53.0	53.8	1.8
18	50.1	52.0	50.6	51.4	51.1	51.0	1.9
19	49.0	50.0	50.2	48.7	48.1	49.2	2.1
20	49.8	51.1	50.4	51.5	49.0	50.4	2.5
21	48.9	50.2	52.8	50.1	50.0	50.4	3.9
22	49.0	49.1	51.6	52.2	48.0	50.0	4.2
23	52.0	50.9	51.4	49.7	50.0	50.8	2.3
24	49.9	49.1	52.6	50.3	50.0	50.4	3.5
25	50.0	48.8	51.5	49.1	51.1	50.1	2.7

$$\bar{\bar{x}} = 50.231 \qquad \bar{R} = 3.356$$

A simple time plot of individual numbers, as shown in Figure 2.1, is meaningful. It gives the analyst a picture in which to visualize the stability of the process. Often, machine critical problems or cycling can be identified with a simple plot. These types of problems should be corrected before SPC is begun.

A frequency bar chart is shown in Figure 2.2.

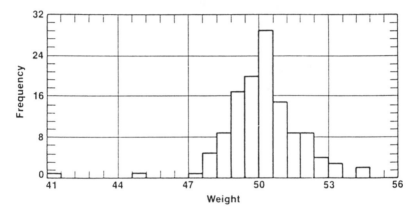

Figure 2.2 Frequency Plot of Bag Weights

This frequency bar plot (histogram) was prepared by one of the popular statistical software packages for a personal computer. Often these software packages are of limited use on the plant floor and have not solved many problems for anyone who did not understand SPC, but for non-real time data analysis and presentation, computer software is a must. * (The March issue of *Quality Progress* contains a complete list of software products).

---

* For a complete list of available software products see *Quality Progress*, 23, No. 3 (March 1990) pp. 54–60.

The $\bar{x}$ control chart for averages is shown in Figure 2.3.

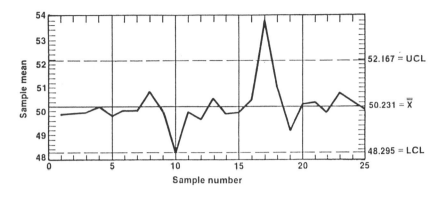

Figure 2.3 $\bar{x}$ Control Chart of Bag Weights

The first point plotted in Figure 2.3 is the first group average of 49.88 pounds. The upper control limits (UCL) and lower control limits (LCL) are based on the average subgroup range $(\bar{R})$ and the average of the averages $(\bar{\bar{x}})$ of Table 2.1, that is,

$$\text{UCL} = \bar{\bar{x}} + A_2\bar{R} = 50.231 + (0.577)(3.356) = 52.167 \quad \textbf{(3)}$$

$$\text{LCL} = \bar{\bar{x}} - A_2\bar{R} = 50.231 - (0.577)(3.356) = 48.295 \quad \textbf{(4)}$$

The A_2 factor comes from the Appendix. The $\pm A_2\bar{R}$ represents the 3σ limits for plotted averages. Sigma represents standard deviation (discussed later). The sample size (n) is five specimens. These control limits are for averages based on five specimens. It is important to adhere to the same sample size on the plant floor. (Five is not a magic number.) As an example, the control limits for plotted individual datum points are over twice as far apart as the control limits of Figure 2.3. (Control limits for individual measurements are covered later in this chapter.) It also is important to note that any calculation based on the average range is not valid when the sample size exceeds 10. (Please do not get bogged down with the calculations! Read on.)

The centerline of Figure 2.3 is the overall process average during the sampling interval. If there is a desired process target, replace $\bar{\bar{x}}$ with this number in Equations 3 and 4. The use of $\bar{\bar{x}}$, versus the desired target, indicates that we cannot produce to target and/or the customer does not care. Typically, neither of these is true. In some cases it may be preferable to plot points that represent deviations away from target. In these situations the $\bar{x}$ chart centerline will be positioned at zero, and the control limits will be at $\pm A_2\bar{R}$ away from the horizontal axis. This approach is useful when many types of similar parts are produced on the same machine during short runs. When the process average is varied, and $\bar{R}$ remains the same, as demonstrated by an R chart (to be discussed later), several production runs of different products can be plotted on the same chart. This technique will be particularly useful if there are sources of assignable cause which can be carried over into the next production run (setup) from a previous type of product. (See the case study at the end of Section 2.10 for a more complete discussion of small lot sizes.)

The typical rules for interpreting all types of control charts are simple. Assignable cause exists and should be investigated:

1. When a plotted point falls outside the control limits.

2. When two points out of three fall in the outer-third zone. (Many people draw in warning limits two thirds of the distance between the centerline and the control limits. This is recommended most of the time. Often it is desirable to color-code the charts. Use red in the areas beyond the control limits and make the warning zone yellow.)

3. When six points in a row are on the same side of the centerline.

4. When obvious trends or cycling exist. The operators can usually tell you about an incremental change between two consecutive points which normally signifies a trend. Four consecutive increases (decreases) often implies a trend also.

Note that no mention is made of customer's plus-or-minus specifications. From Chapter 1 it should be clear that it makes sense only to control a process to its inherent capabilities, or control limits.

From Figure 2.3, we note that subgroup 17 is out-of-control, indicating the presence of some type of assignable cause. Also, with subgroup 10, for example, it is probably safe to assume that the entire process has shifted downward away from 50, as shown in Figure 2.4.

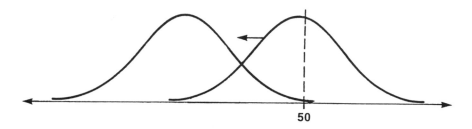

Figure 2.4 Process Average Shift to the Left

If this example represents the beginning of SPC for this process, out-of-control subgroups should be discarded from the data set and the limits recalculated. It is advisable to peruse the data and remove obvious outliers before calculating the initial control limits. If more than 15 percent of the original points are out-of-control, either the sampling frequency is insufficient or the process is too unstable to use SPC at the present. In either case, extensive process analysis is warranted prior to SPC implementation. Out-of-control points should be left on the plot, but they do not factor into the calculations. In the future, the operator takes corrective action and circles the point when it is out-of-control to indicate that adjustments have been made and the job is in order. It is also a good practice to write comments on the charts reflecting corrective actions taken or changes that have been made in the raw materials. On a monthly basis, the charts should be analyzed in a chartroom to identify recurring problems or trends. This is a management function that cannot be avoided. You will find the operators often fail to identify runs above the centerlines or warning-zone messages. Additionally, they often fail to circle points when adjustments are made and do not write in comments. For heretofore stable processes, failure to reinforce these concepts may make SPC not worth the effort. It also is recommended to always calibrate and check out all measurement devices prior to starting SPC sampling.

After several hundred initial plottings, the limits should be recalculated. The original control limits will usually be biased too wide because it is difficult to estimate the limits before the process is stabilized with SPC. Later, when the charts are fully operational, the limits are recalculated only when the charts show that the process consistency (R chart) or centering ($\bar{x}$ chart) have changed at a time when the physical process cannot (or should not) be altered.

As shown in Figure 2.5, a process can be centered, but still contain more variability than can be explained by chance. To monitor the variability of a process away from its average, or centering, range (R) charts are often plotted.

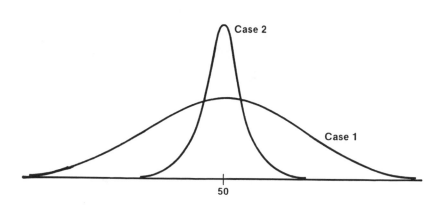

Figure 2.5 Process Centered; Yet Too Much Variability

For the bag weight example, the R chart is shown in Figure 2.6.

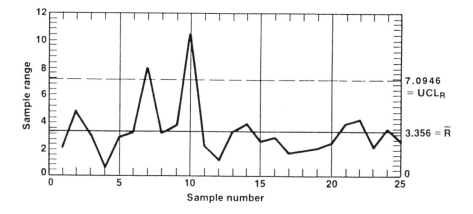

Figure 2.6 R Chart for Bag Weights

The UCL for the R chart is calculated as:

$$UCL_R = D_4\bar{R} = 2.114(3.356) = 7.0946, \tag{5}$$

where D_4 is in the Appendix. If the subgroup sample size is greater than six, a lower range control limit is calculated as:

$$LCL_R = D_3\overline{R} \qquad (6)$$

Subgroups 7 and 10 contain more within-subgroup variability than is expected by chance alone. Therefore, investigation is needed. Perhaps there was a bad analytical measurement or a new batch of raw materials in the middle of the subgroup. In any event, discard subgroups 7 and 10 as outliers and recalculate all the control limits for the $\overline{x}$ and R charts. Ideally you would want to determine why the outliers existed. If the historical production logs are not accurate enough to do so, still eliminate the outliers from the calculations. Since initially calculated limits are based on the data and are often too wide because the process does not have SPC yet, plotted range values just inside UCL should likely be discarded as outliers also during the initial calculation procedures. Anything two thirds the distance to the UCL may initially be called an outlier. Do not use an R chart or $\overline{R}$ for sample sizes greater than 10. If you do, you will get an inflated estimate of the process common cause variability. Before the charts become operational, it usually is recommended to install warning limits two thirds the distance from the target to the control limits on R charts, just as with $\overline{x}$ charts.

With an intelligent use of control charts, a management-operator team usually can eliminate most of the future sources of assignable cause. This is particularly true if some sort of cause-and-effect log and Pareto chart are established. (For a discussion of Pareto charts see the example on page 182.) An in-depth discussion of Pareto charts can be found in Ishikawa (1985).[11]

Doctor W. Edwards Deming indicates that management should not be satisfied in the long run with a process just because there are no sources of assignable variability. The chance variability, or common cause, should also be reduced because any variability costs the customer. It is solely the responsibility of management, however, to reduce the level of common cause, because only drastic process engineering studies will find reasons for previously considered chance variability. A team approach is necessary to make these studies. The team should consist of several process engineers, the department manager, and at least one experienced operator. (See Section 5.1 for a more complete discussion on problem solving.) When the common cause has been reduced, it will show up on an R chart as long runs below $\overline{R}$, or as a reduced standard deviation.

2.2
Statistical Issues Pertaining to Starting X-bar Charts

The following steps generally apply when starting an SPC investigation:

1. Make sure that the process is not broken.

2. Take 25 subgroups of consecutively produced specimens (usually consisting of four to five samples). (This may not apply for continuous or batch processes. See Section 2.8.)

3. Calculate the average range ($\bar{R}$), and $\bar{\bar{x}}$ (if no target exists).

4. Construct the trial limits. (Use $\bar{\bar{x}}$ [not target] to identify initial outliers.)

5. Discard the out-of-control points, often called outliers.

6. Recalculate the limits. Plot all the original data.

Regarding step 5, if four or more of the plotted points are out-of-control, either the time interval between samplings is too wide, or the process is broken and should be repaired before steps 1 through 6 are repeated. One point out-of-control is typical for the first plot. If any remaining points are out-of-control after step 6, repeat steps 5 and 6.

2.3
Subgrouping of Specimens

When plotting $\bar{x}$ charts for discrete processes, each subgroup normally should consist of four or five consecutive specimens. (If sampling and testing is prohibitively expensive, a sample size of one may be acceptable. See Section 2.9.) The $\bar{x}$ control limits are based on $\pm A_2\bar{R}$, where $\bar{R}$ represents the average within-subgroup range. What we want is the distance between these control limits to represent common cause variability which the operators alone cannot eliminate. Note in Figure 2.7 that the ripple represents typical common cause variability, and that assignable cause (local faults) occurred at points 1 and 2. We want to sample only the ripple when estimating $\bar{R}$. We do not want assignable cause to occur within a subgroup.

To maximize the probability that $\bar{R}$ represents only common cause, for discrete processes, subgroup n consecutive specimens for a sample size of n. When accumulating the initial data to calculate the control limits, if the process experiences an unlikely shift within the short time interval of a single subgroup, the plot of this sample range will be out-of-control on the initial R chart and probably will be eliminated before final control limits are calculated.

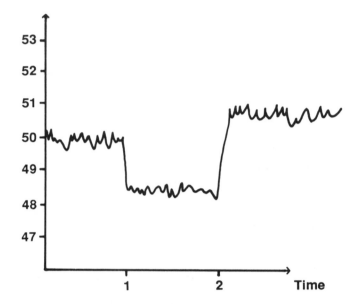

Figure 2.7 Common and Assignable Variability

Theoretically, for processes producing discrete items of production, one should try to sample subgroups of items in a manner that minimizes the variability within subgroups and maximizes the variability among subgroups. Usually four or five consecutive specimens work well. This philosophy does not necessarily apply for continuous processes that do not have discrete items of production.

If we had sampled our five specimens randomly over a long period of time (versus from consecutively produced items), the process could have shifted several times in opposite directions with the highs and lows cancelling each other when paired within the same subgroup. The subgroup range would also represent assignable cause, and thus be too large for a control limit calculation. For example, if we take the data of Table 2.1 and randomly assign them into groups of five rather than group them consecutively, we find that none of the $\bar{x}$ values are out-of-control. Yet, with the proper sampling scheme, we found two averages to be out-of-control, as seen in Figure 2.3. Reread this paragraph if your vendors are providing you with control charts for their shipments to you. Data that are not chronological (first-in first-out) will always appear in control, regardless of what the process is doing!

If several items are sampled during a time period which represents a single lot, however, and if the purpose of the sampling is lot acceptance rather than process control, a random sampling of the entire interval is needed. However, you will find that lot acceptance is not nearly as effective as statistical process control. To have an effective and efficient process from a quality control perspective, the process must be controlled so that the product is made correctly the first time.

2.4
Sampling Frequency

Some operators have a mistaken perception of the process stability because they have interpreted the chance variability as something wrong. Thus, they are uneasy with subgrouping five consecutive items of production to represent the entire sampling interval. They perceive the process as being less stable than the facts support. In the short run, effective processes remain centered and the variability about this average is within the range of expected chance variability. As a rule of thumb, there should be an average of about 20 plotted points between occurrences of assignable cause. After approximately 100 plottings with SPC in effect, the charts can tell you if the sampling interval is correct, and if the process is in a state of statistical control. In the beginning, the best recommendation is a sampling interval that the operators recommend as appropriate.

2.5
The Charts Must Look Correct

A control chart should be maintained by the person who makes the process adjustments, and this person must fully understand the rules listed in Section 2.2. One of the major reasons for charts that look like Figure 2.8 is that supervisors often fail to realize that SPC is an operational tool, just like a wrench or micrometer.

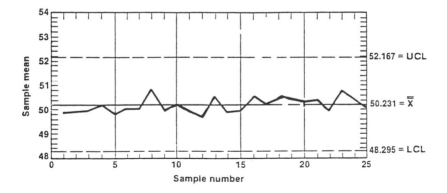

Figure 2.8 Looks Too Good

If operators find that they are being graded on summaries such as percent out-of-control, they naturally will react by taking the best five out of seven specimens, or by simply lying to survive. When the sampling method and interval are correct, there will be a few points out-of-control. Well-trained operators and supervisors view this situation as an opportunity to correct and improve the process. Figure 2.8 looks too good. It may be, however, that SPC and awareness in general have improved the process capabilities to the point that new limits need to be established.

Over the long run, the charts must look correct. You expect to see only about 70 percent of the plottings inside the middle third of the area around the centerline. There should be approximately one in 20 plottings within the warning zone, or the outer third of the interval.

Later sections will contain examples showing how failure to identify the continuous nature of processes also can lead to control charts that do not look correct.

2.6
The Sample Size and Precision

Most users of SPC use a sample size of four or five with success. This sample size is not a requirement. One or two specimens per subgroup may suffice. Ask the operators what they think, or choose a minimum and watch the charts for a month. From a theoretical perspective, however, the choice of sample size should be based on the precision desired. If a shift in the process average of "E" units will harm the customer, the necessary subgroup sample size (n) can be calculated as:

$$n = \left[\frac{(4.28)}{E} \sigma \right]^2 \tag{7}$$

where the sigma (σ) represents the standard deviation of individual specimen measurements. The constant 4.28 is based on the statistical odds relating to the area under the normal curve. The odds are something like this: If the process average shifts by E units from its target, there is a 90 percent chance that the SPC chart will identify this assignable cause with the next plotted point. Also, there is a 99.73 percent chance that assignable cause exists when a point is outside the control limits. Since an SPC chart also can help identify subtle runs off target or trends, over time, the odds actually are better than the formula indicates. This is the reason why a simple sample size of five generally works well with SPC. An estimate of σ can be calculated as:

$$\sigma_{LT} = \sqrt{\frac{\Sigma(x-\bar{x})^2}{n-1}} \qquad (8)$$

by entering the individual datum points into a calculator with a σ function. The best way to estimate the value of E is to determine how far the process limits are from the customer specifications. The process limits are $\bar{\bar{x}} \pm 3\sigma_{LT}$.

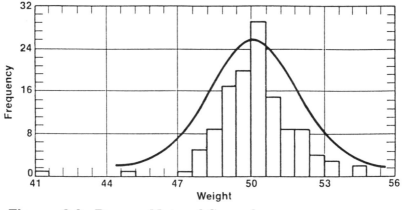

Figure 2.9 Process Natural Spread

As shown in Figure 2.9, a process has some natural spread. It is customary to consider the natural spread of a process to be $\pm 3\sigma$ (standard deviations) from target. To establish E of Equation 7, one may calculate σ, establish Figure 2.9 for the process with some statistical software, and see how far the process average can shift before the outer edges of the bell-shaped curve get too near the customer specification limits, LSL and USL. Formulas for E are, the smaller of USL − ($\bar{\bar{x}}$+4σ), or ($\bar{\bar{x}}$− 4σ) − LSL.

σ also can be estimated as :

$$\sigma_{ST} = \bar{R}/d_2 \, , \qquad\qquad (9)$$

where d_2 values are listed in the Appendix for various subgroup sample sizes. Note that Equation 9 pertains to the average range from many subgroups. One cannot estimate σ from one subgroup.

In either case, the standard deviation or σ represents process variability. Equation 8 will yield total process variability representing all sources of variability, chance, and assignable cause. Equation 9 will be only a representation of the chance variability. The LT and ST subscripts represent long-term (total) and short-term (chance) variability.

$$\sigma_{LT} > \sigma_{ST} \qquad\qquad (10)$$

It is not likely that Equation 7 will be used for sample size determination, but if it is, Equation 8 should be used for estimating σ. Equation 9 will be used for process capability studies to be covered later in this chapter. The difference between σ_{LT} and σ_{ST} gives an indication of how much better you can do when using SPC. Ten to 30 percent improvement is typical.

The control limits for $\bar{x}$ charts are typically based on $\pm$ $A_2\bar{R}$ of the target or the grand process average, $\bar{\bar{x}}$. The average-range technique is only valid for subgroup sample sizes less than or equal to 10. If extreme precision is required and Equation 7 yields a required sample size in excess of 10, the control limits should be based on the average subgroup standard deviation $\bar{\sigma}$. The limits for the average chart are:

$$\bar{\bar{x}} \pm A_3\bar{\sigma} \qquad (11)$$

A σ chart can be maintained to help identify when σ increases. The limits for the σ chart are based on:

$$UCL_\sigma = B_4\bar{\sigma}, \text{ and} \qquad (12)$$

$$LCL_\sigma = B_3\bar{\sigma}, \qquad (13)$$

where $\bar{\sigma}$ is the average of the subgroup standard deviations, each calculated as in Equation 8.

For the data of Table 2.1 on page 25, there are 25 σ_i values for the 25 subgroups. The σ_1 equals 0.926 units. The σ_2 equals 1.99, and $\bar{\sigma}$ equals 1.33 units. The control limits for the average chart are:

$$\bar{\bar{x}} \pm A_3\bar{\sigma}, \qquad (14)$$

$$50.231 \pm 1.427(1.33),$$

$$50.231 \pm 1.898 \text{ units.}$$

The limits for the σ chart are:

$$UCL_\sigma = B_4\bar{\sigma} = 2.0\ 9(1.33) = 2.78 \qquad \textbf{(15)}$$

$$LCL_\sigma = B_3 \times \bar{\sigma} = 0, \qquad \textbf{(16)}$$

where A_3, B_3, and B_4 are shown in the Appendix.

Some measurement devices calculate the standard deviation of the data within each subgroup. There is no minimum subgroup sample size for control limits based on σ, so Equations 11 through 16 can be used in all cases. When applicable, however, the average range technique is easier to calculate and is recommended for discrete processes. (Unidentified outliers have smaller biasing effect when using the average range method.)

When it is necessary to identify extremely small, long-term process shifts, the use of cusum charts may be justified. (Duncan [1974][4] has a good discussion of cusum charts.) Some type of computer software is a must for using cusum charts. Few people have found the extra work of cusum charts to be worth the effort to justify their use over $\bar{x}$ charts on the plant floor. They can be useful, however, for office or laboratory analysis of the long-term behavior of processes or for cases of automated testing in combination with an on-line computer. Cusum charts may be good for an off-line analysis to help identify gradually deteriorating machines or measurement devices. A further technical explanation of cusum charts is beyond the scope of this "how-to" book.

An important concept must be understood in reference to Figure 2.9. The control chart limits are based on the natural capabilities of the process. The $\overline{R}$, or whatever number is used to calculate the control limits, is selected so that the limits represent the process chance variability. Even when the specification limits are within the control limits, in the short-term it is best to respond only to the control chart limits. Trying to force the process to do the impossible will yield a situation such as Figure 1.3. When the process is inherently incapable, it is desirable to inspect many units and screen them based on the customer specifications. However, process adjustments should be made only when the control charts indicate that adjustments need to be made.

Be careful when asking first-line supervisors or operators to calculate the statistical limits. The SPC coordinators or some other technically competent manager should do the behind the scenes calculations. It is sufficient to tell the operators that the control limits are the *natural process limits* representing common cause. They already know this, but don't have the words to express it. Then the operators should be trained through a format similar to Sections 1.0 through 2.5 using data from their process. There will be more discussions on training in Chapter 5.

It is important to motivate the operators to circle the out-of-control points and write in what caused the problem as well as what action they took to solve it. Try to leave room on the charts for comments. Then a monthly chartroom analysis usually will enable management to permanently design many recurring problems out of the process. Many firms overlook this most important step. Not to mention the obvious engineering reasons, a chartroom analysis shows the operators that this SPC is important to management. Otherwise, the charting will probably become after-the-fact over time, done only when there is time to plot, and before the plant manager makes his routine rounds. The letter "C" in SPC means *control.* You have SPC only when the charts are used to control the process in real time. Many so-called SPC programs in industry involve only after-the-fact plotting. There is no *control!*

Another point deserves discussion here. Many high-volume, continuous processes have so many system upsets and operating strategy inconsistencies among the operators that SPC charting is practically useless at the outset. The relevant variable may instantaneously and frequently jump from four σ on the high side to beyond the lower control limit and beyond the apparent control capability of the operators. Most of these issues should be corrected before SPC begins, or at least you must be prepared to level with the operators pertaining to upset conditions when SPC plotting may not help. Pulp and paper mills are ideal examples of this case where it takes at least six months to prepare for SPC.

2.7
Process Capability Studies

Control charts for $\bar{x}$ values (averages) have limits that apply only for plotted average values. Customer specifications are based on individual specimens. To convert the process control limits to be applicable to individual measurements, and thus comparable to the customer specification limits, the short-term standard deviation (σ_{ST}) of Equation 9 is used. The process limits, for individuals, are calculated as:

$$\text{Process Average (or target)} \pm 3\ \sigma_{ST} \qquad (17)$$

where for the data of Table 2.1,

$$\sigma_{ST} = \bar{R}/d_2 = 3.356 / 2.326 = 1.44 \text{ units} \qquad (18)$$

Equation 18 does not usually apply for continuous processes. Read on!

For target weights of 50 pounds, the natural process limits are calculated as:

$$\text{Target} \pm 3\ \sigma_{ST}\ (1.44) \qquad (19)$$

$$50 \pm 4.32 \qquad\qquad \textbf{(20)}$$

As will be discussed in Section 2.9, Equation 17 represents one method for establishing the limits for control charts for individuals. Since σ_{ST} represents the chance variability only, this is the best that the process can perform at present. Using this technique for process capability studies is valid only when SPC is being used to enable the elimination of all assignable causes of variability. There are no exceptions to this rule!

There are several indexes that compare process capabilities to customer specifications. Most of them are statistically invalid unless the process is in-control, which means that 95 percent, or more, plotted points indicate a state of control on the SPC charts. The most common measure of process capability is Cp (sometimes called CPI) defined as:

$$Cp = \frac{\text{Upper Specification} - \text{Lower Specification}}{6\,\sigma_{ST}} , \qquad \textbf{(21)}$$

where the $6\sigma_{ST}$ represents the $\pm\,3\sigma_{ST}$ process best-case capability. Two cases of Cp are shown in Figure 2.10.

Most customers expect a Cp > 1.5 units. This leaves a margin of safety for cases where the SPC efforts may not immediately identify all assignable causes.

The use of Equations 18 and 21 to calculate σ_{ST} and Cp is based on the assumption that the histogram of the data is somewhat bell-shaped and the process is in statistical control. There are also some processes that do not produce bell-shaped histograms even when they are in

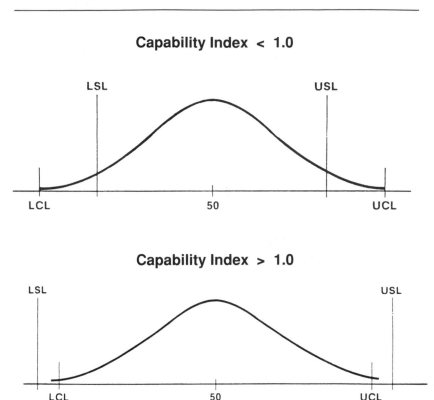

Figure 2.10 Two Process Capability Cases

statistical control. Skewed-to-the-left histograms are extremely rare. Skewed-to-the-right histograms are uncommon, but do occur. Skewed-to-the-right cases naturally have a few data points far to the right of the average with most of the data bunched near a lower boundary, frequently zero. Industrial engineering data relating to machine downtimes and time-to-failure data are examples of naturally skewed-to-the-right data. These types of data can be from several types of theoretical distributions; however, the log-normal distribution is a good approximation for most skewed-to-the-right data. In other words, the natural logs of the raw data probably form a bell-shaped histogram.

To estimate the process capability of a skewed-to-the-right type process, there are two approaches. One is to formulate a histogram of the raw data and by inspection to compare it to the customer's specification limits. The second approach is to transform the raw data by taking the natural logs. Then, by taking the natural logs of the customer's specification limits, the process capability index can be estimated. In either event, C_p and C_{pk} only apply if the process is in-control.

For processes with naturally skewed-to-the-right data, one SPC plotting approach is to always work in the natural log mode by plotting the natural logs of the data. Then the chart has symmetrical limits. Another is to calculate the $\bar{x}$ and 2σ limits from the transformed data in the natural log mode and then to take the anti-logs to give control chart targets and limits that apply to the untransformed raw data. Then the raw data can be plotted on the control chart. The limits will not be symmetrical. (2σ control limits are generally too tight for normally distributed data; however, for skewed-to-the-right data, 2σ upper control limits are much more agreeable to management and seem to work well.)

Another process capability index is called C_{pk}. This index penalizes the producer for having a process average ($\bar{\bar{x}}$) that is not centered in the middle of the customer specification limits. The C_{pk} is the smaller of

$$Cpk \ = \ \frac{\text{Upper Spec Limit (USL)} - \bar{\bar{x}}}{3\sigma_{ST}} \text{, or} \qquad \textbf{(22)}$$

$$Cpk = \frac{\bar{\bar{x}} - \text{Lower Spec Limit (LSL)}}{3\sigma_{ST}} \qquad (23)$$

For the bag weight example of Table 2.1, using a USL of 53 and a LSL of 47.

$$C_{pk} = \frac{53 - 50.231}{3\,(1.44)} = 0.64, \text{ or} \qquad (24)$$

$$C_{pk} = \frac{50.231 - 47}{3\,(1.44)} = 0.75 \qquad (25)$$

When $C_{pk} < 1.0$ and the process average cannot be adjusted to correct the problem, or when $C_p < 1.0$ (indicating an incapable process), SPC will enable you to do the best you can in the short-term. SPC will generally provide a 10 to 30 percent improvement in process capability. In the long-term, however, major process engineering changes probably will be necessary. Pressure on the operators to do the impossible will only make the problem worse by forcing them to overcontrol as in Figure 1.3, or by making liars out of them. A $C_{pk} < 1.0$ is a long-term process engineering problem. Pressure tactics by management are a short-term alternative that will not work for this long-term problem.

It is important to note that for continuous processes discussed in Sections 2.8 through 2.13, the average range is typically not a good representation for the process common cause when the subgroups cover a short production interval. There are several approximate methods for estimating process capability ratios for continuous processes. None of them are very good! One technique is to establish a histogram, as in Figure 2.2, of the process while it is in control. Then the process capability ratios can be established by inspection. A better technique is the use of the pooled standard deviation plugged into Equations 22 through 25. (See Section 2.9 for a discussion of the pooled standard deviation.) Another technique is to completely randomize the data for a period, to subgroup the numbers into pairs, to calculate the average range, and then to establish the process capability ratios through Equations 18, and 22 through 25. For completely randomized data, the within-subgroup ranges should represent process common cause if outliers are eliminated previously with an R chart. In Equations 22 and 23, if σ_{ST} is replaced with σ of Equation 8, this is called PPK and may be used as a long-term measure of quality performance. The process performance index, PPK, will be about 20 percent less than C_p if the process is in control. C_{pk} is applicable only when the process is in statistical control. PPK always is applicable. PPK also is applicable for data naturally skewed to the right.

2.8
Continuous Processes (The Bag Example)

From the bag example of Section 2.1, it was explained that a batch of ceramic mix would feed the line for about four hours. The operator samples five successive bags every 30 minutes. In the process block diagram of Figure 2.11, the dark squares represent bags from one batch and the light squares correspond to specimens from the next (or previous batch) of ceramic mix. Note the sampling of subgroups of five:

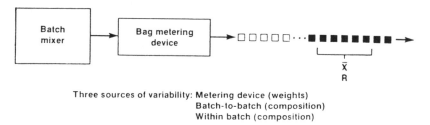

Three sources of variability: Metering device (weights)
Batch-to-batch (composition)
Within batch (composition)

Figure 2.11 Ceramic Bagging and Mixing Process

In the bagging process discussed earlier, each successive specimen usually is a discrete independent unit pertaining to weight. Therefore, the ranges from within the subgroups likely will represent the relevant short-term process chance variability for bag weights. The control limits based on $A_2\overline{R}$ are correct in this case for discrete items of production. However, if the measured variable were percent composition, successive bags would not be independent specimens, because in most cases several bags in a row will have the same constituents if the batch is well-mixed. Remember, a batch lasts four hours. Five successive specimens represent only a few seconds. There will be about 30 minutes between plotting of the averages, and in some cases a new batch will be in the system between two plotted averages. Consequently, the average subgroup range ($\overline{R}$), representing only a few seconds, does not truly represent the variability expected among plotted averages from different batches. The $\overline{R}$ represents within-batch variability, not between-batch variability as seen on the control chart among many plotted $\overline{x}$ values. From a theoretical perspective, the within subgroup data for continuous processes present the situation where the data points are correlated among themselves, thus not independent. This is called serial auto correlation and is discussed by Montgomery (1985). [16] The method outlined below is an approximation which usually is recommended on the plant floor. For off-line analysis of process data where statisticians with computers are involved, the more theoretical treatment may be recommended.

There are several ways to approximate the limits for a batch-continuous process. The most straightforward is to simply calculate the standard deviation of the $\overline{x}$'s. The calculations from Table 2.2 indicate this technique for percent binder in the bags of composite ceramic powder mix. The standard deviations of the averages or $\bar{x}$ column is called $\sigma_{\bar{x}}$ and equals 0.0105 (from the calculator) for the data of Table 2.2. The $\bar{x}$ control limits are:

$$\text{Target} \pm 2.33\,\sigma_{\bar{x}}\,,\text{ or} \qquad (26)$$

$$\text{Target} \pm 0.024. \qquad (27)$$

An R chart can be maintained, but it must be remembered that any plotted subgroup range represents mostly some combination of *within-batch* and measurement system variability. (The 2.33 factor gives control limits for 98 percent confidence. This choice of confidence is based on empirical experience.)

When using Equation 26, it is important to guard against *outliers*. An outlier is a number outside of $\bar{\bar{x}} \pm$ 1.645σ which should be omitted when estimating the standard deviation for future use with control charts. The use of 1.645 versus the more conventional 2σ or 3σ case seems too drastic, but it is not. It is common for the initial SPC limits to be too wide. Prior to SPC there is always excessive process variability. To the best of your ability, the variability that can potentially be controlled through SPC charting should not be used in establishing the initial limits. (For discrete processes, the normal rules of Section 2.1 apply for identifying outliers, since a direct calculation of σ is not used.) This later portion of Section 2 contains a large variety of continuous processes, at least one of which probably is similar to your case.

Table 2.2 Percent Binder Data for Composite Ceramic Bag Mix

Subgroup	Subgroup Data					$\bar{x}$
1	.15	.17	.20	.13	.19	0.168
2	.17	.20	.15	.17	.15	0.168
3	.16	.15	.17	.14	.16	0.156
4	.14	.16	.15	.13	.16	0.148
5	.16	.17	.15	.16	.17	0.162
6	.16	.15	.17	.16	.17	0.162
7	.15	.16	.13	.17	.16	0.154
8	.16	.17	.15	.14	.18	0.160
9	.17	.20	.20	.12	.17	0.172
10	.16	.17	.13	.15	.17	0.156
11	.14	.17	.16	.17	.15	0.158
12	.17	.20	.17	.15	.18	0.174
13	.15	.14	.16	.17	.15	0.154
14	.30	.15	.20	.20	.15	0.200
15	.16	.20	.13	.13	.14	0.152
16	.17	.19	.15	.14	.16	0.162
17	.16	.17	.16	.15	.17	0.162
18	.15	.17	.15	.17	.16	0.160
19	.16	.17	.13	.14	.15	0.150
20	.15	.14	.15	.20	.14	0.156
21	.13	.17	.15	.16	.17	0.156
22	.17	.16	.14	.15	.16	0.156
23	.16	.17	.13	.15	.16	0.154
24	.17	.15	.13	.20	.17	0.164
25	.13	.14	.17	.16	.17	0.154

$$\sigma_{\bar{x}} = 0.0105$$

2.9
Control Charts
for Individuals

Another alternative for this batch bagging process is to sample only one specimen from each batch every four hours. Then a control chart for the individual measurements can be maintained with limits calculated as:

$$\text{Target} \pm 2.07\,\overline{MR}, \qquad\qquad (28)$$

where $\overline{MR}$ is the average moving range. The moving ranges that are averaged are calculated as the difference between measurements one and two, two and three, etc. (The 2.07 provides 98 percent confidence.) See Table 2.3 for a new example.

Basing decisions on individual measurements is risky for several reasons. First, the precision is low (based on Equation 7), and the process average can shift drastically without being noticed. Second, there is no opportunity for measurement system variability to get averaged out before the plotting. In any event, control charts for individuals often are used as an effective method of process control.

This method of plotting control charts is advised for accounting data or sometimes for samplings from a continuous chemical process where there is no rational subgrouping into collections of four or five specimens. Also, the average moving range technique and a chart for individuals normally work well for railcar to railcar shipment data, etc.

Relating to the example of Table 2.3, the use of an SPC chart in the front office is the best beginning of a quality improvement effort. An example like Table 2.3 would be a good starting place. When in-control, only upper management can improve the system. When out-of-control, immediate pressure to find the local faults probably will be effective. These last two sentences sum up the profound knowledge of W. Edwards Deming, and should be memorized by all managers.

The control limits are:

$$\bar{x} \pm 2.07\,(\overline{MR}) \text{ or } -6.6 \pm 4.60 \qquad (29)$$

For convenience, only 10 data points were used. In practice, 100 or more should be employed. Twenty-five observations may suffice temporarily. In these cases, however, label the limits and chart as "tentative." As always, be careful of outliers in the initial calculations.

The previous example of SPC for a front-office type variable is from real data. Note that the accounting variable is in control, but not acceptable (hence, not centered on zero with narrow ± variability). Since it is in control, the problem is not a local fault attributable to the operators or supervision. There is a deeper system problem that only management can solve. Most likely, the budgets were unrealistically established in an absence of statistical thinking. A major challenge of the future for SPC practitioners is to help management learn to use control charts to separate local faults from system problems. In reality, the first charts should be in the front office.

Table 2.3. Dollar-Value Labor Variances

Month	Dollar Variance	Moving Range
1	-8	$1 = 8 - 7$
2	-7	2
3	-9	4
4	-5	3
5	-8	5
6	-3	2
7	-5	1
8	-6	1
9	-7	1
10	-8	

$$\bar{x} = -6.6 \qquad \overline{MR} = 2.22$$

For continuous chemical processes, the control limits based on $\pm 2.33\sigma_{\bar{x}}$, as discussed in Section 2.8, may be preferred over the average moving range technique. This is especially true if the time interval among the samplings seems small enough, such that representative measurements of total process common cause do not occur between successive data points. If this is the case the distance between the control limits will seem too narrow. In these cases, the example explained below provides a useful alternative. When the average-moving-range technique is acceptable, it may be desirable to keep a range chart also, especially for continuous processes. The operators are aware that too much of a change between two consecutive specimens often indicates that the process is trending in the revelant direction. An out-of-control condition on an R chart may help make this clearer. Another simpler alternative is to define as a trend any deviation larger than $D_4\overline{R}$ between two consecutive specimens.

Another technique that may be useful for continuous processes is to calculate the standard deviation of the individual checks. Before the plus-or-minus control limits are established, for plotting purposes, however, it is extremely important to identify the single measurements containing assignable cause. An example follows in Table 2.4 for the percent moisture of ammonium nitrate product from a continuous chemical plant. Based on empirical experience, you should use 2σ limits when working with continuous processes, with individual datum points and a direct calculation of the standard deviation. A direct calculation of the standard deviation yields a result that often is biased upward. Consequently, 2σ limits will appear more realistic than the usual three standard deviation control limits. The confidence is somewhere between 95 and 99.73 percent, depending on how accurately the outliers are eliminated, and how appropriate the sampling interval.

It is important to note that at times the operators can beat the charts in continuous processes where there are lags between the time an adjustment is made and the time the total effect takes place. If they are acting in advance because their intuitive knowledge is a natural part of the process, let them do so. If they are wrong, a subsequent chartroom analysis of the charts will reveal it.

Table 2.4 Percent Moisture

Hour	Percent Moisture
1	2.5
2	2.5
3	2.7
4	2.4
5	2.6
6	2.5
7	3.3
8	2.5
9	2.4
10	2.5

$$\text{Target} = 2.5$$
$$\sigma = 0.264, \text{ and}$$
$$\text{Target} \pm 1.645\sigma = \tag{30}$$
$$2.5 \pm 0.434$$

With 90 percent confidence, the reading of 3.3 (an outlier) likely indicates assignable cause that the other data points do not, since it is outside the 1.645σ limits. The 1.645σ range is used to identify outliers for continuous processes when Equation 31 is used for control limit calculations. The control limits will be based on 2σ. In any event, we are 90 percent sure that something was different about the process at the time the percent moisture was 3.3 percent. Recalculating the standard deviation without the 3.3 datum point yields:

$$\sigma = 0.093,$$

with the 2σ control limits as:

$$\text{Target } \pm\ 2(.093), \text{ or } 2.5 \pm 0.186 \qquad \textbf{(31)}$$

Note how much smaller σ is with the one outlier discarded. The smaller σ is more correct.

When using the average moving range technique of Equation 29 for individual specimens from a continuous process, it is seldom clear whether the sampling interval is correct so that the moving ranges yield the correct control limits for the plotted numbers. For the moving range technique the control limits are based on $\pm\ 2.07$ $\overline{MR}$ from Equation 28. The average variability between pairs of data should be representative of the chance deviations one expects to see among the plotted points on the control chart. Often it is not clear whether or not the moving ranges contain assignable cause, or if two consecutive samplings are independent specimens. Consequently, if control charts for individuals are necessary for economical or logical reasons (as with accounting data), and if the plotted charts do not appear correct based on the comments of Section 2.5, use the direct standard deviation technique from the previous percent moisture example. Pay close attention, however, to outliers.

To prevent long-term, gradual assignable cause from inflating the calculated standard deviation, often it is advisable to stratify the data into days or weeks and then to calculate the strata variances to be averaged (pooled). As an example, if 24 hourly specimens are taken daily, you may calculate the daily variances (S_i^2) eliminating outliers as in the previous percent moisture example. Then the standard deviation to be used in the control-limit calculations would be

$$\sigma_p = S_p = \sqrt{\frac{S_1^2 + S_2^2 + \ldots + S_{30}^2}{30}}, \qquad (32)$$

for 30 days of data. Once again, with this method, or any other based on a direct calculation of standard deviation, it is essential to eliminate data points with assignable cause or measurement error. One erroneous number out of 20 can inflate the calculated standard deviation drastically.

2.10
Job Shop, Small Production Quantity Case

In the cases of short production runs, classical SPC may be of limited value. When this appears to be the case, management or important customers need proof and an alternative approach to quality improvement (control). A data-based approach is used to manage these issues.

For the job shop it does not make sense to plot, as an example, $\bar{x}$ and R points on a chart on a frequent basis when several orders (thus, setups) occur between plottings. Unless you can feasibly plot six points within an order so that process adjustments can be made in real time to improve the quality of the rest of the order, the most beneficial approach is to concentrate your efforts on understanding how to more effectively make the setups, assuming there will be future orders for this product. Most management, and all operators, frown at the necessity of this approach because they have not distinguished between common cause and assignable variability, thus believing that every setup for a specific product must be different. Generally this is not true. Experience has shown that operators usually will not converge to the optimum setup by trial and error. The time planning horizon and data analysis skills of the typical production operator are such that they do need help from management pertaining to the precise machine setup to yield a desired product output.

To prove this point, on many occasions, companies have taken 20 (or more) production orders of the same product with five data points evenly spaced throughout the orders (subgroups). For a job shop, one would expect the within-subgroup (within-order) variability to be considerably smaller than the variability from order to order. In other words, the machine is fairly consistent from the beginning to the end of the order. The total variability of the 20 orders (100 specimens) usually can be expressed as:

$$\sigma^2 \text{ (total)} = \sigma^2 \text{ (within-order)} + \sigma^2 \text{ (among-order)}. \text{ (33)}$$

The σ^2 (total), or total variance, can be estimated by using Equation 8 with a calculator which has a σ function. The σ^2 (within-order) can be estimated by using Equation 9 as $\overline{R}$, where $\overline{R}$ is the average range of the 20 subgroups. It is typical to find 60 to 90 percent of the total variability explained by order-to-order (thus, setup-to-setup) variability, and probably no statistically significant within-order variability. This order-to-order variability comes mostly from operator-to-operator differences and *changes in recipes* of the same operator over time. This statistical analysis is strongly recommended to capture the attention of the manufacturing personnel.

When the aforementioned statistical analysis yields the typical results, we can refer to these types of processes as setup-critical (versus SPC-critical). The next step is to find a procedure for identifying the best setup for each product. (As a warning, however, this may not be feasible unless the raw materials are in a reasonably good state of statistical control.)

With the same finished product data used to establish the aforementioned components of variance analysis, and assuming there is a synchronized production log of machine settings, the data matrix is partitioned such that only the best five observations are considered. Then for these five data points the average ($\bar{x}$) and σ are calculated for each machine setting. If any data fall outside $\bar{x} \pm 2\sigma$, these numbers are discarded and the average recalculated. These average machine settings are used as the initial optimum setup.

Then it is explained to the operators that they are requested to try this setup, with the SPC coordinator present. The SPC coordinator initially stays with the process to take full responsibility. In a controlled fashion, the SPC coordinator may take the advice of some operators to experiment with slight deviations from the scientific setup. After it has been proven to work, through a group meeting, the SPC coordinator discusses the results to elicit buy-in from the operators.

There may be cases where the machine settings (variables) are so highly interactive that this procedure might not work. In these cases, a multiple regression analysis or EVOP, with the help of a statistician, must be used (Ryan, 1989).[17] The simple approach, however, seems to work well 19 out of 20 times.

In the case of a job shop where orders are not recurring, or do not repeat themselves, precontrol or the multiple regression approach may help. (See the following example.) Never use the first-item inspection method, based on one measurement, unless your customer's expectations are low and he is uninformed or unconcerned about quality.

In the job shop where extreme customer pressure exists to use SPC charts, perform the aforementioned procedure first to install scientifically based machine setups. Then set up charts with a minimum of one plotted point per order. The SPC charts may help you fine-tune your setup formula, however, you probably will find that the charts will perform only a political function.

A detailed numerical example follows (Fellers, 1990).[5]

The Problem

This study involved a case where a small vendor sold corrugated boxes to a large customer who had high quality expectations for their suppliers. About 30 percent of the vendor's product was purchased by this large customer, so meeting their needs and keeping their business was an economic necessity. The large customer had been successful with statistical process control (SPC) and other more advanced multivariate cause-and-effect studies. Consequently, they asked this vendor to use SPC on all his processes and to be able to prove in subsequent audits that their processes were in statistical control. They were instructed to produce to target according to the teaching of Geneci Taguchi (Scherkenbach, 1986),[18] instead of simply staying in specification. There had been, however, little historical evidence of the vendor's product being out-of-spec. The vendor also was asked to demonstrate, on a semi-annual basis, how they were using statistics to *continually improve* according to the teachings of W. Edwards Deming (1986).[2]

A basic problem existed, however. The customer had applied statistical techniques to their high-volume, continuous processes, and did not fully appreciate the fact that the vendor's corrugated box business was more of a job shop. On any given eight-hour day, approximately 20 different order types were run on each machine. Since different orders typically correspond to drastically different shapes and sizes of boxes, each run on the factory floor required the operators to completely disable the flexing-printing machine and to readjust all of the dozen, or so, machine settings before start-up. A typical run length was one hour, so an operator could not plot more than one point on a control chart during this period, unless the manning level was increased. A control chart alone would have been an inefficient, and likely ineffective, means of controlling this process. Many empirical studies have shown that SPC charts alone do not enable one to effectively control an industrial process unless at least six points can be plotted and responded to in real time before the run is over. In a job shop, however, a control chart can provide a historical quality assurance (QA) record of the fact that the product tested was acceptable, and that the machine setup was apparently correct. This is merely documentation however, not real-time quality control.

The essence of this empirical study was the determination that the most efficient and effective use of statistics (SPC) was to establish a method to enable management to provide the operators with a road map for more effectively setting up the machine. It was found that if the machine was optimally set up at the outset of a new order, the quality would be good and there was little need to check any product after-the-fact, or during the run. In this case, like most of the others analyzed over the last decade, the optimal setup remained constant over time for the same product as recurring orders were processed. The operators, or management, initially were suspicious of this fact. A large part of this project involved a methodical approach to establishing *buy-in.*

Before this method is explained, several other approaches to quality assurance (QA) relating to after-the-fact inspection of small batches will be reviewed. These other approaches may suffice, but getting-by no longer is sufficient. In any small lot-size situation, the essence of good quality is to know how to optimally set up the process, not how to inspect product after-the-fact. To statistically establish optimum setups, however, the nature of a business must be what the plant management called a pseudo-job shop. A pseudo-job shop exists when there is repeat business for a product, even though the typical order size is too small for conventional SPC charts. Empirical process settings and corresponding quality data from the historical repeat orders are used to help statistically oriented managers find the near-optimal setups for future business for this specific product. In a pure job shop consisting of custom, one-time jobs, this study does not apply.

It is seldom acceptable to use *first-time inspection* as a sole QA technique for a job shop. The infrequent exceptions are when it is known that every item in a production batch is identical, hence no common cause variability, or the process capability index is greater than 2.0 and in-house specifications are used that are at least 1.5 times narrower than the customer's requirements. Both of these situations are rare (especially the former). One can understand the fallacy of first-item inspection by viewing Figure 2.12.

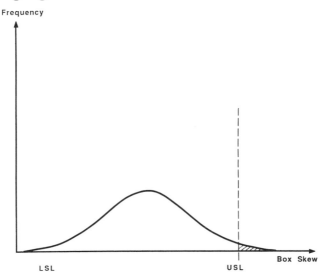

Figure 2.12 Fallacy of First-Item Inspection

As an example, note in Figure 2.12 that there will be occasions where a significant part of the batch is outside the USL when some of the product is acceptable. Even worse, many operators are pressured to keep retesting until an acceptable specimen is found. Consequently, no batches ever fail unless the percent defective is 100 percent! In today's marketplace, the process (production lot) average should be at the target, which is normally midway between USL and LSL, or at some mutually agreed upon location for one-sided specifications. First-item inspection seldom delivers this level of quality control.

A slightly more effective version of inspecting initial specimens from a small batch currently being produced is precontrol. There are several versions of precontrol. A typical approach may be:

1. Divide the customer's specification width in half. Designate Zone A as a region nearest the centered target. Zone B areas are the regions outside Zone A, but still within specifications. Zone C is the region outside either specification limit.

2. Start the job.

3. If the first piece is in Zone C, reset the machine and repeat step 2.

4. If the first piece is in Zone A, check the next four pieces. If all five are in Zone A, make the rest of the job.

5. If the first piece is in Zone B, check the next piece. If this second piece is in Zone B or C, reset the machine and repeat step 2. If this second piece is in Zone A, check the next four pieces. Start the run if five in a row are in Zone A; otherwise, repeat step 2.

Precontrol is acceptable as a last resort for job shops, either as an interim measure while management is searching for a more appropriate preventive technique, or when all else fails. To convince operators to accept precontrol after years of first-item inspection requires demonstrated commitment by all levels of management, plus some statistical training related to common cause and the message of Figure 2.12.

A slightly more statistically valid, but infrequently used, approach to precontrol for small lot sizes would be to inspect n specimens from the beginning of the batch to test the hypothesis that the process (product) average is not statistically significantly different from a specified target. If the feedback from the testing cannot occur before the majority of the batch is produced, the analyst must take n random specimens from the batch to make a decision about acceptance of the lot. The sample size, n, should be established as:

$$n = \left[\frac{3.24\,\sigma}{E} \right]^2, \qquad (34)$$

where σ is the estimated standard deviation, which represents the common cause variability of the process. The E-factor represents the required precision, which is the amount the process average can deviate from the specified target before the customer will have quality problems. The value of E should be the smaller of:

$$\text{USL} - (\text{Target} + 3\,\sigma\,), \text{ or} \qquad\qquad \textbf{(35)}$$
$$(\text{Target} - 3\,\sigma\,) - \text{LSL}.$$

The value 3.24 in the above formula came from a z-table and 5 and 10 percent producer's and consumer's risks, respectively. In other words, there is a 5 percent risk of failing a good lot and a 10 percent risk of passing a marginal batch with a few defectives (likely parts per million). The procedure is to test the first n items. Calculate the following:

$$t = \frac{\overline{x} - \text{Target}}{\sigma/\sqrt{n}}, \text{ where} \qquad\qquad \textbf{(36)}$$

the average ($\overline{x}$) and standard deviation (σ) are calculated from the data of the n specimens. If the t-value is less than 1.96, release the process and continue to produce the rest of the batch, or accept the lot if it is already produced. If the t-value exceeds 1.96, make the necessary process adjustments and repeat the entire procedure with n new specimens. The disqualified lot must be screened at 100 percent, or scrapped.

The use of any type of precontrol or first-item inspection, if applicable, as a QA/QC procedure requires that the process be stable enough such that the remainder of the produced batch has the same average and variability as the initially inspected items. On an experimental basis, this can be proven by checking every item during some runs of orders that are of a typical quantity. As discussed below, however, it is common, if not practically universal, in job shops relevant to this paper on small lot sizes, for the process to remain stable during the entire production run.

Classical SPC charts can sometimes be used for small order job shops by plotting deviations from target on the graph with zero as the centerline. Then, by looking at a chart covering many orders, one can establish the long-term quality that the process has been producing. To use this technique as a QC procedure, however, the within-order standard deviations for different types of product must be similar, so that the same control limits apply from order-to-order. From an assortment of typical orders covering the full range of at least a dozen product types, no single within-order standard deviation should be more than 30 percent different from the pooled standard deviation of all the orders. If this requirement is met a deviations control chart always can be useful as a QA tool to document the fact that the product was acceptable during the charted period. As a quality control tool to provide preventive analysis in the real time, however, these charts are of limited process-control use unless there are quality issues that can exist as local faults from order-to-order (across orders), e.g., deteriorated process components or exceptionally bad raw materials. Either of these situations may cause consistent statistically significant runs above (below) the control chart centerline of zero, across several different orders (setups). Most of these types of conditions, however, develop over such a long period that one may need to analyze a large number of chronological charts to see any trends. An off-line chartroom analysis or CUSUM may be recommended (Duncan, 1974). [4]

A More Appropriate Method for Pseudo-Job Shops

For pseudo-job shops where orders for many of the product types are recurring, you usually find that the within-order variability is negligible when compared to the order-to-order variability. What this means is that if the process is set up properly and the raw materials are acceptable, the product will be good, and there is little need to check product after the fact. Consequently, management's efforts should be to help establish the optimum setup, by product type, such that the process average is inherently on target from order-to-order. This approach also will limit operator tampering which will reduce variability. All orders over time will be the same, and the customer will be able to run his process with no incoming inspection or batch-to-batch process adjustments. This consistency will help the customer to use JIT to reduce inventories.

For the flexing-printing process under discussion, the operators were heretofore incorrectly convinced that for the specific product, there could not be a universal group of process settings (setup) that would apply in all cases over time. As the following discussion shows, we proved them wrong. Their initial disbelief resulted from our failure to provide statistical training so that they understood the concept of common cause variability of the incoming raw material, of the measurement system, and of their finished product. They perceived every random deviation to constitute a needed process adjustment. Eventually we provided this training, but not until we had a road map to enable them to establish, with our help, the optimal setup for each order type. Now, as a result of the following work, they believe the basic quality axiom, "When the raw material processes are in statistical control, the same process in this department produces the same result every time." (Except for common cause, which temporarily must be ignored.)

Most of the statistical work was performed behind the scenes so that we could prove our method before asking for operator buy-in. Our first statistically related goal was to prove that the majority of the long-term assignable variability was order-to-order (among-order) versus within-order. This would prove to the operators that if all the setups were the same, all the product would be identical, except for common cause. It also would show that for our order sizes, once the process was properly set up, the quality would remain consistent, making within-order or among-order tampering unnecessary and inappropriate.

To begin with, we obtained finished product data from 24 historical customer orders of the same product. Five random specimens had been tested per order to yield 120 total observations. An analysis of variance (ANOVA) was performed with order number as the qualitative independent variable and skew as the response variable.

(The skew quality variable is a measure of box squareness.) The target is zero, but about 3/32 inch is the best the machine can perform. Variability in skew causes the customer to have to continually adjust the automatic folding and packaging machine to prevent jam-ups. When his packaging machine jams, his entire production line is stopped. The ANOVA table is shown in Figure 2.13. No attempt was made to explain Figure 2.13 to the operators.

SOURCE	SS	DF	MS	F	PROB>F
Setup (order)	1052.4	23	45.8	12.44	0.0000
Residual	353.2	96	3.7		
Total	1405.6	119			

Figure 2.13 ANOVA Table for Setup-to-Setup Variability

An analysis of Figure 2.13 enabled the quality management staff to conclude the setup-to-setup variability was statistically significant with a confidence level of 100 percent. It was shown that 69 percent of the total variability could be attributed to setup-to-setup variability. This was established via a components of various analysis (Ryan, 1989). [17] Equation 33 would have yielded similar results. The operators temporarily accepted this fact and were receptive to the idea that the best way to improve the consistency of the product supplied to the customer was to minimize or reduce the order-to-order inconsistencies. The only method for doing this was to set up the process in the same manner for recurring orders. An analysis by the operators of the plus-

and-minus standard error bars for order (setup) averages in Figure 2.14 further established operator buy-in. It was clear that consistency from setup-to-setup should be the goal of our QC efforts, not the typical approach of trying to *jawbone* the operators into paying closer attention or trying to *inspect quality into* the product with some kind of forced SPC charting.

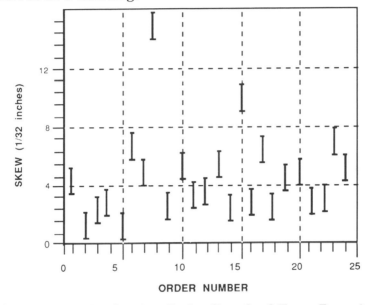

Figure 2.14 Production-Order Standard Error Bars, in Chronological Sequence

Now the quality management team began developing a behind the scenes plan to help establish a method for the determination of optimum groups of machine settings for each product type. One experienced operator was on this team to provide advice and to help establish subsequent operator buy-in.

The quality variable of particular interest was box skew. A histogram of the data for the 120 observations, covering 24 orders is shown in Figure 2.15

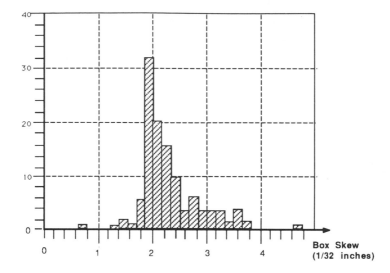

Figure 2.15 Histogram of Skew Variable

An analysis of Figure 2.15 could lead one to believe that during the six-month production interval there was a stable statistical (stochastic) system with one average (mean) and only common cause variability. An analysis of Figure 2.14, however, clearly shows that over time the data did not come from one statistical population. In the long-run, the process was clearly out-of-control, and the local fault was the setup variability from order-to-order. Discussions with the operators made it clear that this variability was a combination of day-to-day, crew-to-crew, operator-to-operator, and within-operator sources of deviations. The important issue relating to Figures 2.14 and 2.15 was, "How was the machine set up when the skew variable was small (thus good) versus how was it set up when the quality was marginal?" As shown below in the subsequent analysis, the groups of machine settings that gave good quality from order-to-order were similar. The same applied for the cases of marginal quality. The important issue was that the group of settings that gave good quality was different from the group that gave bad quality, with a small amount of overlap.

The next, but optional, analysis step involved a multiple regression using the same historical finished product data and the corresponding machine-setup data. Only three out of the dozen variables proved to be statistically significant as shown in Figure 2.16. The adjusted R-square was also a low 2 percent. The independent variables, PR2, SSPR, and CH, of Figure 2.16 are the machine settings: pressure-roll 2, slotter-scorer pull roll, and creaser head. There were nine similar additional process machine-setting variables.

INDEPENDENT	VARIABLE	COEFFICIENT	STD.ERR	T PROB>T
Constant	2.32	0.044	52.56	0.0000
PR2 * SSPR	− 405.57	186.400	− 2.18	0.0309
CH * SSPR	79.85	34.232	2.33	0.0208

Figure 2.16   Regression Results for Skew Regression Machine Settings

The specified functional form for the multiple regression was a polynomial containing all first-order individual terms and all second-order interproduct terms. The interproduct terms were included to quantify the interactions among the machine settings. There was no theory to help us specify a more scientific functional equation. Perhaps this fact, along with the large amount of raw material common cause variability, or the poor precision of the measurement system, could explain the poor statistical fit when using multiple regression. There were no synchronized data for the raw material variables for this six-month period that could be correlated with the finished product skew data. Consequently, all of the large amount of raw material variability was residual in the regression model, and thus substantially increased the probability of Type II errors.

If the multiple regression equation had been accurate, with care we could have used partial differentials to determine the optimum set of machine settings. This technique requires the help of an experienced statistician.

From a purely experimental design perspective, it would have been advantageous to run some controlled fractional factorial experiments to determine the best machine settings. This was not a viable alternative for two reasons. First, to meet their production schedules, management was not able to let us have the process for several days to run all the experimental conditions, many of which likely would have generated defective product. Also, we were skeptical about using a highly fractionalized design since the interactions would not have been identified. Multiple regression analysis with the historical data had previously helped us appreciate that interactions among variables were the norm, rather than the exception. An evolutionary operation (EVOP) was not allowable because to successively experiment in small steps would have taken years, since the typical product is only made an average of twice per month.

A simple approach to finding the optimal setup is to subset the data set, shown pictorially in Figure 2.15, into the worst and best quartiles. In this case of box skew the best would have been the lowest 25 percent of the data and the worst would have been the highest 25 percent. Then one can calculate the averages and standard deviations for each machine setting for each subset of data. For each machine setting then, a t-test or simple qualitative comparison of the average settings for the good quality, versus the marginal, could show if the results were definitive such that the machine setting averages for the best quartile could be recommended as the near optimal process settings. This procedure, however, would be recommended only if there was a shortage of computational resources, such as professional statisticians and computers. In our case this was not the situation. We decided to use cluster analysis to help establish the process near-optimal machine settings for this product.

Cluster analysis is a multivariate statistical technique generally used by marketing executives to help them identify their target markets. Considering typical demographic variables such as age, income, or educational level of customers for one of a firm's products, there are generally fairly homogeneous groups of people (clusters) that do, or do not, purchase the item. The object of cluster analysis is to locate the relevant clusters so that the firm can target its advertising and promotion to, or away from, the interesting groups.

As an example, cluster analysis would certainly show that mostly affluent 30- to 45-year-olds buy BMWs. Consequently, why price or promote the product for people in their early 20s? Also, why promote or design it for older people. The marketing package for the BMW is correctly recognized as "too expensive for non-Yuppie types," and "too exciting for wimps." Mathematically, the computations behind cluster analysis are far beyond the scope of this text. With a computer and a reasonably good multivariate statistical software package, however, cluster analysis is simple to use.

Our application of cluster analysis in this QC environment was quite different. Our dependent variable was box skew, versus sales, as in the classical marketing examples. Our independent variables were the machine settings, versus a demographic characteristic such as age or income. The computer output of one of the more definitive cluster analyses is shown in Figure 2.17.

The circles were generated by the computer to enclose the different clusters. The machine settings within a cluster gave similar skew results. In other words, the within-cluster variability was low, and the among-cluster variability was high. In this case, it was obvious that the cluster in the lower right gave the best finished product quality where the skew was minimal. We took the average of the pressure roll 2 machine settings in this cluster as our initial near-optimal level for this setting. It would have been tempting to take the individual datum point for pressure roll 2 that gave the lowest value for skew. This technique, however, would not have considered the common cause variability (stochastic nature) of the finished product variables. To quote W. Edwards Deming: "One number tells you nothing!"

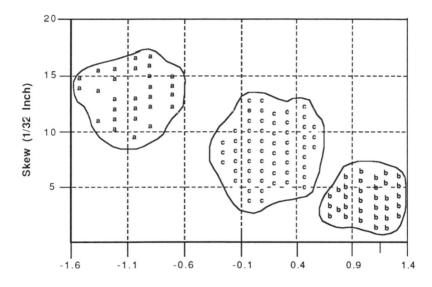

Figure 2.17 Clusters for Pressure Roll 2 Setting

The clusters for the slotter-scorer pull roll are shown in Figure 2.18.

Several of the clusters for process settings were not completely definitive. As shown in Figure 2.19 for the feed roll machine setting, the same setting at times gave good, average, and marginal quality.

For the several cases like the one of Figure 2.19, the experienced operator on the team helped us decide what the initial near-optimal machine settings should be.

Subsequently, we experimented with these adjustments upon initial use of our near-optimal machine settings. In reference to Figure 2.19, it was likely that the multivariate, interactive, and stochastic nature of the situation masked the individual (main) effect of these few machine settings. Luckily, there were only three out of the 12 settings where the results were not definitive. It was these three process settings that the operators said had little effect on the box skew.

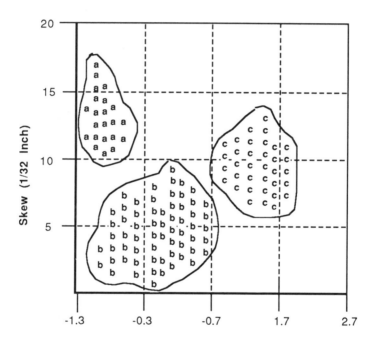

Figure 2.18 Clusters for Slotter-Scorer Pull Roll Setting

At this point, for this product, we had a set of initial near-optimum machine settings. For communications purposes, we named them the *good-run settings* for this product. The next phase was to introduce the good-run settings to the operators and to try using them on the plant floor.

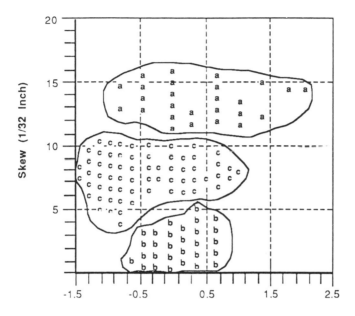

Figure 2.19 Clusters for Feed-Roll Setting

Implementation

The ultimate result of this study was a listing of the good-run settings on the route sheet that accompanied the order to the flexing-printing machine. Exact machine settings would be specified, not ranges within which the operators could tamper. When the operators found it necessary to deviate from the good-run settings, their explicit changes are documented on the route sheet and a copy sent to the quality manager. Periodically the quality manager would analyze the deviations to establish if the machine had deteriorated, or if the good-run settings needed adjusting. Prior to statistically analyzing the process, the route sheet only contained the finished product specifications. It was the operator's responsibility to produce in-spec product. The results of Figures 2.12 and 2.14 were what was happening prior to the use of good-run settings, and the customer was having to compensate for this variability by making annoying adjustments to his automatic packing machine.

At this point in time, however, the operators who were not on the good-run settings analysis team were still suspicious that the machine could be set up exactly the same over many months to produce the same product. We had felt that it was necessary to perform all the investigative statistical work off-line without any fanfare, unless an operator asked what we were doing. One operator, however, was on our think tank team. Our upcoming implementation phase was designed mostly to educate the employees and to elicit buy-in.

To begin the implementation training, we gave the operators approximately two hours of SPC training to make sure that they understood the concept of common cause in the process, in raw materials, and in their measurement system. The thrust of this training was to enable the operators to think of a datum point as a member from a statistical distribution, instead of an absolute. We also taught them how to maintain an SPC chart. Control charts were installed on this process at this point, not as a primary real-time control procedure, but (1) for political reasons related to customer audits, (2) to provide a long-term check on machine wear, (3) to fine-tune the good-run settings if the operators' remarks on the charts indicated that it was necessary to deviate from the near-optimum machine settings, and (4) to provide a spot-check for catastrophic process failure. It is interesting to note that after about a year, items 2 and 4 have not required operator follow-up. Item 3 was interesting when a new product was first subjected to the new good-run setting philosophy. After several orders (setups), however, few adjustments were made to the good-run optimal settings. Only one point per order could be plotted on the control charts because of the short duration of the runs. Hence, there was no real-time SPC.

The next phase of the operator training was an explanation of the ANOVAs of Figures 2.13 and 2.16. We wanted to prove to the operators that among-setup variability was the major controllable local fault. We also made it clear that it was a failing of management that had caused this excessive variability. We explained that their jobs revolved around eight-hour blocks of time, and that they were previously performing just as they had been instructed. That was, "At the outset of an order, get it in spec. Then pay attention to the product and adjust the process when you feel it is necessary." Management had not provided the long-term summaries as in Figure 2.14, nor had it previously provided the expert statistical help to establish a methodology for determination of the good-run settings. This second phase of the training lasted about two hours, and we were careful to let them know that management was doing something for them, not simply asking them to "do better," without a road map to change the system.

Several days later, in the third training session, we explained the concept of good-run settings with discussions of the clusters as shown in Figure 2.17. Perhaps there could have been a more straightforward up-front statistical approach to obtain the good-run settings, however, the results of the graphical cluster analysis of Figure 2.17 were easier for the operators to understand. For the first several products that we had analyzed, we gave them the good-run settings. They were still a bit suspicious, so we told them that during the initial applications of the new technique, the SPC coordinator would be on the floor and would take full responsibility. It also was explained that the initial good-run settings could be adjusted slightly during the first several uses, but only in coordination with management. For the relevant products, the new setup philosophy started the next day. We also started the SPC plotting at the same time. For comparison purposes we had been sampling for this continuous process for several months before the application of statistics. Note on Figure 2.20 that the average and the variability were greatly reduced at point 120 on the horizontal axis, which was the time that the good-run settings and SPC charts were begun for this product.

The operators were impressed immediately. They felt that they now had a tool to enable them to produce to target. Management had finally accepted the fact that the operators alone could not change the system to improve quality.

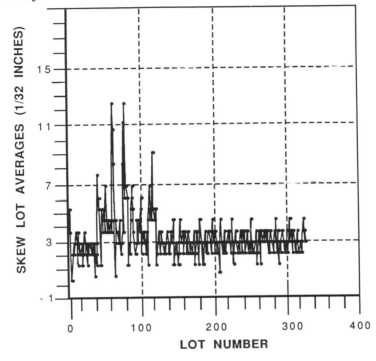

Figure 2.20   Before and After Results

Conclusions

In this case it surprised everyone (except the author) that in a pseudo-job shop the process should be set up exactly the same every time there was a repeat order for a product. The case described here was typical of most situations. The same message was clear in this case as in the others. Management cannot simply provide the operators with specifications and walk away from the technical process implying to the production operators that quality is their responsibility. Either classical SPC, statistically established good-run settings in a pseudo-job shop, or an optimum process recipe based on EVOP or some other type of response surface analysis must be provided by management.

2.11
Continuous Processes (An Extruder)

In an extrusion process, there is a constant stream of molten material forced through a die of a certain profile or shape. After a new die is verified as having the proper shape or dimensions, there still will be some chance variability and possible assignable cause variability in the profile or cross-sectional shape of the product. Some of the assignable cause comes from changes such as temperature shifts or changes in the raw material mix. Chance variability, of course, comes from unexplained sources, many of which likely result from raw material variability.

An extrusion process can be both continuous and discrete within an SPC setting. If standard lengths of product are cut to customer specifications, the cutting process is discrete, making control limits based on $\pm A_2 \overline{R}$ correct for plotting charts based on averages. In the cutting process the chance variabilities of successive units are usually independent. However, the cross-sectional profiles of successive units are not independent. Two consecutive cuts of product may best be explained as one big piece cut in two when looking at cross-sections. For any reasonable subgroup size, the within-subgroup variability will be much too small to represent the chance variability expected among the plotted averages on the control charts. The plus-or-minus limits based on the $\pm$ $A_2\bar{R}$ will usually be about two to three times too narrow. The control chart may look like Figure 2.21 even when the process is in its best state of control. This is because the short-term variability from a subgroup of consecutive or closely spaced specimens does not fairly represent the longer-term batch-to-batch variability in raw materials, to name only one source of common cause variability.

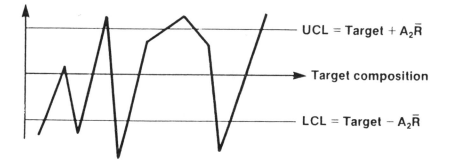

Figure 2.21 Control Limits May Be Wrong

It is a good idea to sample four or five consecutive specimens to average-out analytical imprecision. Then the control limits for plotted averages should be based on $\pm$ 2.33 $\sigma_{\bar{x}}$ as in the example of Section 2.8, while paying close attention for outliers, or initial points outside of the initial trial control limits.

2.12
Continuous Processes (Paper-Making Machine)

A block diagram for a paper-making machine is shown in Figure 2.22. A sheet of paper approximately 10 feet wide is continuously delivered from the process. Rolls of product are cut and wrapped every hour or so.

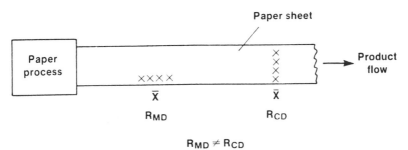

Figure 2.22 Paper-Making Process

A typical sampling technique involves taking several layers of product from the end of each roll. In effect, since the roll circumference is approximately 20 feet, the process is sampled every 20 feet or so as shown by the horizontal x's in Figure 2.22. The comments from the example of Section 2.8 apply here. The control limits for an $\bar{x}$ chart should be calculated directly as $\pm 2.33\sigma_{\bar{x}}$ since this is obviously a continuous process, even though the hourly roll-up may make it appear otherwise. It is advisable, however, to use subgroup averages of four or five specimens to enable the measurement and sample-preparation imprecision to be averaged out. Note that the time sequence of the sampling in this case is in the direction of product flow, often called the machine direction (MD). The within-subgroup ranges likely represent analytical imprecision, not process common cause. It is advisable to resample when an R-value is out-of-control.

Another sampling method is represented by R_{CD} in Figure 2.22. From a single sheet, the cross-direction (CD) variability is sampled. Typically this is recommended in addition to the MD sampling. However, care must be used in the calculation of the limits and interpretation of the charts. Plottings of the $\bar{x}$ values represent a time sequence of the process for an instant. The variability among plotted averages on the control chart represent machine direction variability. This chart can be used to fully represent the state of control of the process in the machine direction. It is recommended that the limits be based on $\pm$ 2.33 $\sigma_{\bar{x}}$ as explained in Section 2.8 for the bag example. The within-subgroup ranges (R_{CD}) represent cross-direction variability and must not be used in $A_2\bar{R}$ type calculations for the control chart representing machine direction process variability. An R chart can be used, however, to monitor CD controls.

There are many processes analogous to the paper-making example, e.g., coating or sheet-steel operations. An example follows in the next section. Even though $\bar{R}_{CD}$ may not initially equal zero, it may be common for an $\bar{R}_{CD}$ to never be out-of-control. If this is proven with temporary SPC charts, CD sampling may not be a requirement. Steps must be taken, however, to periodically make $\bar{R}_{CD} \cong 0$.

2.13
Paper Machine Example

For the paper machine, or any process that produces a sheet or film with machine (MD) and cross-direction (CD) sources of variability (which are different), it is generally advisable initially to sample across the sheet in four to eight evenly spaced locations. Then control limits based on:

$$\text{Target} \pm 2.33\sigma_{\bar{x}} \tag{37}$$

can be used for the $\bar{x}$ chart and machine direction (or longitudinal) control. As an example, pages 103 through 105 are daily data sheets from a paper machine. (In reality, you need 20 days.) Note that on the first day, the standard deviation of the averages ($\sigma_{\bar{x}}$) equals 30.31 units. The first step for day 1 is to calculate $\bar{x} \pm 1.645\ \sigma_{\bar{x}}$ from the original data to help us identify the outliers during this day. In this case,

$$996.1 \pm 1.645\,(30.31) \tag{38}$$
$$946 \text{ to } 1046.$$

It is not unusual to find one outlier, but in this case we did not. Outliers based on $\pm 1.645\sigma_{\bar{x}}$ should be discarded and the $\sigma_{\bar{x}}$ for this day recalculated. Then the overall $\sigma_{\bar{x}}$ for the 20 days would be:

$$\sigma_{\bar{x}} \text{ (overall)} = \sqrt{\frac{\sigma_{\bar{x}_1}^2 + \sigma_{\bar{x}_2}^2 + \sigma_{\bar{x}_3}^2 + ... + \sigma_{\bar{x}\,20}^2}{20}} \qquad (39)$$

For the present case,

$$\sigma_{\bar{x}} \text{ (overall)} = \sqrt{\frac{(30.31)^2 + (32.268)^2 + ... + \sigma_{\bar{x}\,20}^2}{20}} \cong 30$$

$$(40)$$

It is normally advisable to initially keep a range chart to determine if there is assignable cause across the sheet. The overall R-bar is the average R for the 20 days. For each of the 20 days, an upper limit of $D_4\bar{R}$ ($2.114\ \bar{R}$ in this case) is used to identify the R values that should be discarded in the subsequent calculation of the new limits. The $D_3\bar{R}$ value for the lower control limit is zero, since $D_3 = 0$ for sample sizes less than 7.

Many papermakers and film producers will state that they have no control over the variability across the sheet. This is not true. The common cause across-the-sheet variability cannot be eliminated unless more accurate, special controllers are installed specifically to control in the CD direction. If assignable cause is indicated with an R chart, however, a needed process adjustment can be identified. This process change may be expensive and disruptive.

(Note that in this case the $\pm$ control limits for averages based on $A_2\overline{R}$ [which is wrong] are ± 130. The correct limits are closer to $\pm 2.0\ (30)$, or ± 60.)

VARIABLES CONTROL CHART (X̄ & R)

PART NAME (PRODUCT)	Machine Direction Strength
OPERATION (PROCESS)	Paper Machine #1
OPERATOR	Sue
MACHINE	#1
PART NO	DAY 1
SPECIFICATION LIMITS	1000 ± 250
UNIT OF MEASURE	Gr.
ZERO EQUALS	—

$\bar{\bar{X}} = 996.1$

$\sigma_{\bar{x}} = 30.310$

$\bar{R} = 231.88$

SAMPLE MEASUREMENTS	1	2	3	4	5	6	7	8	9	10	11	12	13	14	15	16	17	18	19	20	21	22	23	24
1	850	1030	990	900	890	990	805	1100	1060	850	1050	1150	950	1000	850	1080	890	820	930	820	890	825	1100	1060
2	1030	1060	1060	750	905	1000	950	1100	960	900	1020	900	900	1130	950	800	1030	830	920	1060	1020	1010	1030	930
3	1070	1150	1000	1030	1100	1200	1050	1000	930	1090	1010	990	1100	890	1050	890	800	1100	999	1090	930	1020	835	850
4	930	960	920	1050	1005	1105	1030	890	1040	1020	950	1030	1110	900	1100	890	1040	1110	1120	900	1030	1040	975	1100
5	990	980	950	930	1190	950	930	920	1010	905	930	1110	1150	905	1190	1020	1050	1030	1140	925	1120	985	980	1050
SUM	974	1034	1006	972	1018	1049	953	988	949	1002	1034	1047	965	1028	946	962	946	1021.8	1025	1008	996	984	998	
AVERAGE X̄	974	1034	1006	972	1018	1049	953	988	949	1002	1034	1047	965	1028	946	962	1021.8	1025	1008	996	984	998		
RANGE R	220	190	160	150	300	250	245	210	160	220	190	260	250	240	340	280	250	280	220	260	230	195	265	250
NOTES																								

AVERAGES: 1200 1100 1000 900 800

$UCL_R = 478$ 450   350 $\bar{R} = 226$ 250

RANGES

$\bar{R} = 226$

1200 1000 800

VARIABLES CONTROL CHART (X̄ & R)

PART NAME (PRODUCT)	OPERATION (PROCESS)	PART NO	CHAR
Machine Direction Strength	Paper Machine #		

OPERATOR: B.11 MACHINE: #1

SPECIFICATION LIMITS: 1000 ±250
UNIT OF MEASURE: Gr
ZERO EQUALS: —

$\sigma_{\bar{x}} = 32.268$

$\bar{R} = 225.42$

	1	2	3	4	5	6	7	8	9	10	11	12	13	14	15	16	17	18	19	20	21	22	23	24
DATE																								
TIME																								
1	980	1100	930	1110	830	930	980	870	1010	1010	920	920	1000	890	930	1100	860	920	1130	875	920	860	1210
2	1010	1000	890	1100	850	850	1050	980	1030	1020	1020	1080	870	1100	1100	1200	875	1020	1120	1000	975	1105
3	1010	950	1100	950	1010	1100	1130	1130	1020	1010	1200	1130	1100	1120	1120	1105	925	1100	1200	1030	970
4	970	980	1200	1010	1100	1200	1080	1100	890	1630	1030	1010	1010	1050	1630	870	930	1000	945
5	890	1010	980	890	1150	980	920	890	940	980	1190	980	1650	860	890	925	1010	1020	930	920	970	850
SUM																								
AVERAGE X̄	974	1008	1020	1012	954	1046	980	998	974	1012	1008	1072	990	970	1010	1072	948	1014	1000	1009	1016	969
RANGE R	130	150	310	210	270	350	220	240	160	330	100	230	270	230	230	215	160	170	260	395	160	170	360
NOTES																								

AVERAGES scale: 1200 · 1100 · 1000 · 900 · 800

$UCL_R = 478$

RANGES scale: 450 · 350 · 250

$\bar{R} = 226$

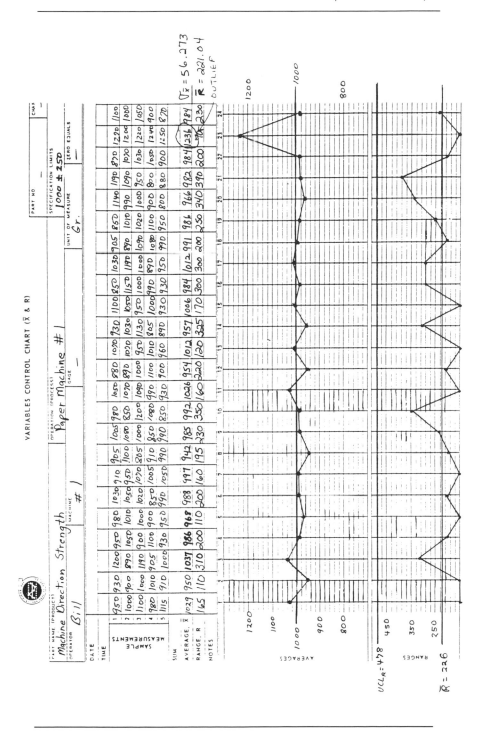

2.14
SPC When There Is a Single-Sided Specification

Because most of the SPC formulas seem to be only for plus-or-minus types of situations, many managers fail to see that there is little difference for single-sided specifications. A classic example is the kaolin processing industry. Kaolin is a white clay that is mined and then processed into a white powder or slurry (looks like toothpaste). The basic process involves cleaning the trash (iron and grit) from the clay, adjusting the moisture, and providing the final viscosity that the customers desire, if in slurry form. An important product variable to most customers is the amount of remaining sand (grit) in the product. There is only a USL for grit, which is typically 0.3 percent. It is simple to decrease the amount of grit in the finished product by leaving the product in the centrifuge longer and/or by increasing the RPM of the centrifuge. Either alternative, however, reduces the process yield. Consequently, the managers had instructed the operators to run the maximum yield, but not to go over the upper specification limit for grit. (This is like telling a motorist traveling 55 MPH to speed up; but don't get a ticket!) The lab technicians also were told to resample a batch if the first specimen was out-of-spec. A graphic representation of what the customer saw is shown in Figure 2.23.

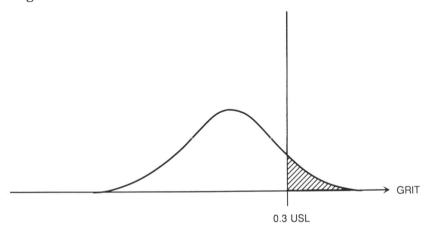

0.3 USL

Figure 2.23 Keep It Large, But Stay Below USL

Upon further analysis, we find that the true distribution looks more like the one of Figure 1.3. Depending on which squeaking wheel was heard last — customer complaints or failure to meet the production standards — the flustered operators were tampering (overcontrolling) the process. It is clear that stabilization of the process could have enabled the producer to stay within spec and run a high yield. In any event, for the following case, after the customer got his process into statistical control and began to more accurately identify the effect that the absolute value of grit and the variability had on his process, the message became clear to the kaolin producers. "No out-of-spec product, and use SPC to control to a specific target." The desired net result was that of Figure 2.24.

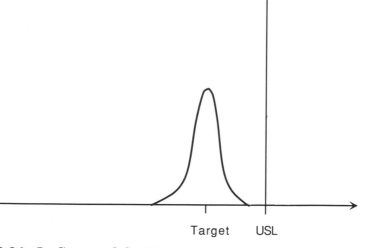

Target   USL

Figure 2.24 In-Spec and On-Target

Notice the margin of safety above the 3σ limit. The customer wanted the target to be 4σ below the upper spec limit to yield a C_{pk} = 1.3 units.

The first step was to identify the true σ. As usual, with the operators previously being forced to tamper, the apparent σ was likely 25 to 50 percent larger than the true σ resulting from common cause. A crude SPC chart was initially located at the machine with a target of 0.24 percent and estimated control limits at ± 0.05 from thecenterline. These limits were a first-guess based on some historical data. Then the operators were asked not to adjust the process unless there was clear evidence of an out-of-control condition. The resulting data are shown in Table 2.5.

Table 2.5 Grit Measurements

Hour	Percent Grit
1	0.19
2	0.23
3	0.27
4	0.26
5	0.28
6	0.16
7	0.22
8	0.23
9	0.28
10	0.26
11	0.25
12	0.27
13	0.27
14	0.25
15	0.21
16	0.23
17	0.26
18	0.28
19	0.27
20	0.25
21	0.18
22	0.23
23	0.25
24	0.24
25	0.23
26	0.27
27	0.22
28	0.26
29	0.24
30	0.25

$$\sigma_{\overline{x}} = 0.0298$$

The control limits to be used in the future were estimated based on:

$$\bar{x} \pm 2.33\ \sigma_{\bar{x}} \tag{41}$$

$$0.243 \pm 2.33(.0298)$$

$$0.243 \pm 0.0694$$

$$0.1736 \text{ to } 0.3124$$

None of the original data were outside of these limits, so it appears that the process was in-control. The process average needed to be adjusted downward, however, since the UCL was above the upper spec limit. The customer wanted the target to be 4σ below the upper spec, so the target was adjusted to:

$$0.30 - 4(.0298) = 0.181 \tag{42}$$

The resulting control limits were:

$$0.181 \pm 2.33\ \sigma$$
$$0.181 \pm 0.0694 \tag{43}$$

$$0.112 \text{ to } 0.250$$

It took careful training of the operators and foremen to persuade them to buy-in to this new philosophy. The trainer rallied around the message of Figures 2.23 and 2.24 with real data to make his point. It did not work. We later found that the operators always ran near the UCL. After 20 years of being told to run on the edge (which in reality is impossible) it was difficult for them to change.

We had to retrain them, and the plant manager had to provide a testimonial of why this was necessary. He had to state in no uncertain terms that we *would* control to a target of 0.181 by using SPC charts.

This process was like many continuous processes. There were causative variables upstream which could significantly reduce the variability in grit at this point near the end of the process. We should have stabilized these upstream variables first, but we did not for political reasons. The customer wanted SPC on the finished-product variables as soon as possible.

At this point, we accumulated synchronized production-log data to run a regression analysis to determine which upstream variables were most correlated with grit in the final stages of the process (Ryan, 1989). [17] We found that approximately 35 percent of the variability in grit could be attributed to the variability in the clay moisture entering the centrifuge. This moisture was controllable upstream in the process. We put an SPC chart on the upstream variable to stabilize it. This reduced the σ of the finished-product grit by about 15 percent, from a standard deviation of 0.0298 to 0.0253. Consequently, the target could be moved up by 15 percent from 0.181 to 0.208 percent. The new finished-product grit control limits were:

$$0.208 \pm 2.33(.0253)$$
$$0.208 \pm 0.059 \qquad \textbf{(44)}$$

Stabilizing the upstream variability allowed recovery of some of the yield that was lost earlier by asking the operators to reduce the throughput to remove more grit. There also were some additional savings in the lab because there was no further rechecking of suspect lots. There were some labor savings on the manufacturing line too because the operators were no longer forced to waste time tampering with the setup. Additionally, process engineers were able to more effectively experiment with the process since it was stabilized by SPC. From a cost perspective, the SPC was an almost break-even situation. Yield was lost, but other dollars were saved. The customers were elated since this kaolin firm had beaten all the others to the punch. Now the kaolin producer can charge a premium for their product. Net result: better quality and more profits!

When there is a single-sided spec, the C_{pk} calculations of page 53 are somewhat different. Only one side applies, either Equation 22 or 23. If the analyst is using SPC software, the C_{pk} calculations may be in error. As an example, in the aforementioned case the USL is 0.3, and there is no LSL. Some computer programs would incorrectly set the LSL equal to zero with the preferred target at 0.15, midway between LSL and USL. For quality reasons it is preferable to be nearer the single spec limit for efficiency reasons, or as far away as possible from the spec limit. In either case, the analyst may have to trick the software by programming in an imaginary specification limit for the nonexistent case. This imaginary specification would be the same distance from $\bar{\bar{x}}$ as the real spec limit.

2.15
Target May Not Be Midway Between the Customer's Specs

Generally it is accepted that the SPC target is midway between the customer's specification limits. If the process moves off target, there is less risk of producing out-of-spec product. Also, for mechanical types of products when tolerance stack-up is an issue, the customer wants the vendor to produce to target (at center) so these parts will fit properly with adjacent mechanical members. For continuous (or discrete) processes involving chemical products, however, a centered target may not always be necessary. The situation of Figure 2.25 may be satisfactory, or even desirable from a cost perspective. With concurrence from the customer, consistency about any target may be the important issue. Tampering or sloppiness is seldom acceptable, although consistent manufacture about a non-centered target (as in Figure 2.25) may be desirable. To repeat, the customer must be involved in this decision.

Consider as an example a firm making an industrial chemical, whose composition is such that it is a liquid at room temperature. Specific gravity is an important variable to most customers. Typical upper and lower spec limits are 38 and 42 for LSL and USL, respectively, as shown in Figure 2.25.

The vendor can rework the product by simply adding water in the final holding tank if the specific gravity is too high; however, if the specific gravity is too low, the product is scrap. The vendor does not have the capability to drive-off water from the product to increase the specific gravity. Consequently, the vendor runs his process near the high side of the specification range. Prior to SPC and stabilization of the process, this type of behavior is common to provide a needed margin of safety for the producer's excessive variability. Consequently, the first step is to implement SPC about *some* target to stabilize the process. With the resulting lower variability, producing to a centered target with no risk of being outside either specification is possible. However, if the centered target is not a possibility from a cost perspective, it may be beneficial for all parties to choose a noncentered SPC target and to stabilize the process with control charts to this target. In many cases, consistency is more important than the long-term average. Owning-up to this fact and stopping the vendor from tampering (overcontrolling) or hiding data may provide better quality. There should be a clear agreement, however, between customer and vendor.

If it is obvious that a noncentered target is preferred, there are two methods for establishing the SPC target. The easiest is to set the target at a distance 4σ from the least costly customer specification limit. This will give a $C_{pk} = 1.33$. Use of this method, however, assumes that the process will be precisely controlled with SPC. If this assumption is risky, place the target 5σ away from the relevant specification limit. A preferable method is to locate the optimum target by using the following formula:

$$\text{target optimum} = \text{LSL} + \frac{\text{USL} - \text{LSL}}{2} + \frac{\sigma^2}{\text{USL-LSL}} + \frac{C_L}{C_u},\,(45)$$

C_L and C_u are the cost per unit of a part being below the LSL or above the USL, respectively. In cases like the present example where the cost of being below LSL is considerably more than that of being above USL, this formula may locate the target within 3σ of a specification limit. This is unlikely, but if it does occur, the target should be located 3σ from the relevant specification limit.

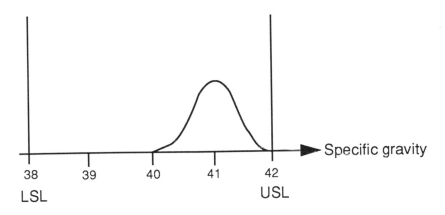

Figure 2.25 Below LSL Is Scrap: Above USL Is Rework

As a side issue for the chemical producer, it was found that in-process SPC not only enabled them to produce to a lower target than was once felt possible, it also enabled them to reduce their total costs. Having to run to the high side of the specification range was mostly a result of the producer's poor method of sampling. The production from one full day went into a holding tank. Then the product from a holding tank was pumped into a finished-product tank that held four days' production. Their sampling was from the finished-product tank on a daily basis. When the specific gravity of the daily product checked was low, they would intentionally run the process on the high side so that the material soon to be blended into the finished-product tank would raise the average of the product to be shipped. When the sample from the finished-product tank appeared on the high side, they would dilute it with water. Both of these compensating actions were expensive, especially running the process on the high side to compensate for earlier produced material that was on the low side. When the in-process specific gravity was intentionally made high to compensate for low measurements in the finished-product tank, the process yield was poor because the compounds tended to precipitate-out and had to be recycled through the system. The total answer was to sample the product from a spigot in the line prior to entering the four-day holding tanks. Then the product and process were being monitored in the real time. The SPC target could be set anywhere because if the process began to drift it was identified within several hours, versus a day or more later.

The scenario in the previous paragraph is typical. Many industrial processes and sampling procedures were designed prior to 1980 when little (or no) statistical expertise existed outside the universities or corporate ivory towers. The SPC analyst must make every attempt to improve finished product consistency and process efficiencies. Often this does not happen. The manufacturing staff receives generic SPC training and is led to believe that all one has to do is plot the existing data. This approach rarely works!

When there are several processes feeding into one holding tank, as in the previous example, it almost always is desirable to use real time, responsive SPC on each process before the product enters a common holding tank.

2.16
One Feed into a
Holding Tank

Related to a physical plant similar to the previous section, the question frequently arises whether to sample the input or output of a holding tank when there is a continuous feed of product from the process into the tank, and finished product (to someone) is taken from the holding tank intermittently. Many producers claim that it is best to sample the product as close to the customer's shipments as possible since this is what he or she receives. For political reasons, e.g., certificates of analysis, this may be true. However, such certificates are dinosaurs which should disappear soon from most vendor–customer relationships. The object is to control the process and correctly manufacture the product. Then the customer can audit the vendor's SPC and other methods to confirm that the product quality will always be good. (After-the-fact control charting of shipment data is not SPC; it is simply a report card.) SPC involves controlling the process at the point of manufacture. Consequently, relating to the questions of where to sample, the correct place is the feed *into* the holding tank or, even better, upstream in the process immediately at the point of manufacture. Using this measure ensures that what goes into the holding tank always will be of good quality because the process will be controlled.

When the holding tank has a capacity of many hours (days) of product, it is tempting to not worry about the actual process since there is substantial blending before the product is sold. With the exception of some aggregate materials which can separate when agitated, it is true that complete blending is common and that this does reduce the finished product variability. However, it is not reduced to zero. Each time you blend n units, the resulting variability is $\sigma/\sqrt{n}$, where σ is the variability with no blending. (As an example, consider the data of Table 2.6.)

This is approximately one day's production. Assume that the holding tank is filled with four days of production before shipments are made. With a typical one-day $\sigma = 0.149$, the usual standard deviation within the tank would be:

$$\sigma/\sqrt{n} \ = \ 0.149/\sqrt{4} \ = \ 0.0745 \ ,$$

where $n = 4$ for four days' product in the tank. The variability is halved, but is not zero. The average pH in the tank is not assured unless the process average of the product entering the tank was controlled with SPC or through automatic controls. Considering the C_{pk} formulas of Equations 22 and 23, blending makes it easier to show finished product results indicative of a capable process. However, if there are long process runs above

Table 2.6   Continuous pH Data

Hour	pH
1	6.9
2	7.1
3	7.0
4	7.4
5	6.8
6	6.9
7	7.0
8	7.1
9	7.0
10	7.1
11	6.9
12	6.8
13	7.0
14	7.1
15	7.2
16	6.9
17	7.2
18	7.2
19	6.9
20	7.0
21	6.7
22	7.1
23	7.0
24	6.9
25	7.0
26	7.0

$\sigma = 0.149$

(below) target resulting from poor process control, the customer still will not be satisfied. Net result: Blending is no excuse for poor process control. Use SPC upstream in the process at the point of manufacture. Not only will quality be more consistent, the total costs of sampling and controlling usually will be less. In extreme cases, it may even become unnecessary to staff the QA lab which has heretofore tried to inspect quality into the product.

The comments of this section also apply to the situations where several feeds enter a common holding tank.

2.17
Several Processes Within a Process (The Rotary Fill)

The picture of Figure 2.26 is typical of many continuous-batch type industrial processes. The vials (containers) on the conveyor are filled with material from a revolving rotary whose six chambers are filled from a common source of input material. The previous process (not shown) is a batch system. Periodically a new batch of feed material is mixed (produced). This type of process is typical in the pharmaceutical and consumer products industries where individual container quantities are important. This applies to boxes of detergent, tubes of toothpaste, bags of potato chips, vials of glucose, etc. Stabilization of these types of processes can save millions of dollars when the producer realizes that they can stay above the lower specification limit with considerably less overpacking. Note that there are several sources of variability to be accounted for and/or controlled. These are chamber-to-chamber, batch-to-batch (upstream), within-batch, and over-time.

The SPC program and control chart limits must be established considering all sources of variability, at least temporarily until the upstream batch variability can be

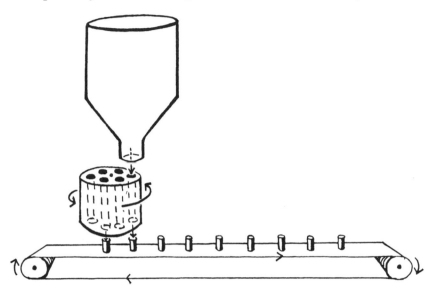

Figure 2.26 Rotary Fill: Process Within a Process

minimized. Blindly following generic formulas and sampling plans is not likely to work well here. If the batch-to-batch variability is low, and if the chamber-to-chamber (consecutive vials) common cause variability is relatively large as compared to the over-time variability, the conventional SPC formulas based on $\pm A_2\overline{R}$ (where R is among chambers) accidentally may work satisfactorily. These conditions, however, are not usual. In the short-run the SPC limits must reflect all the uncontrollable sources of variability. Then after the process is stabilized, the process engineers must eliminate the sources of variability one at a time. This continual improvement will require months and years to complete. Meanwhile, SPC is used to make the product as predictable as possible.

If one followed the standard rules of rational subgrouping and calculations based on $\pm A_2\overline{R}$, the average range among consecutive vials probably would be too small to represent a true proxy for the total process common cause. The control limits would be too tight since $\overline{R}$ represents only common cause chamber-to-chamber variability, which probably is small. The within batch, the over-time, and especially the batch-to-batch common cause variability are not represented by $\pm A_2\overline{R}$. Consider the data of Table 2.7. The column (BA) refers to the batch number.

From Table 2.7, if one incorrectly calculated the control limits for an $\overline{x}$ chart based on the conventional formulas using $\pm A_2\overline{R}$, the control limits would be:

$$\text{Target} \pm A_2\overline{R}$$
$$\text{Target} \pm .483\,(.264)$$
$$\text{Target} \pm 0.128 \ \text{oz.}$$

This is incorrect in this case. Note that there were five batches of raw materials used during the sampling interval. The $\overline{R}$ only accounts for within-cylinder variability, and if these other sources are uncontrollable, at this time, they are common to the system and must be figured into the control limits. An analysis of variance showed that there was statistically significant batch-to-batch variability. [See Ryan 1989][17] for an excellent discussion of analysis of variance, as well as a more theoretical discussion of SPC in general.

Table 2.7 Rotary-Fill Data

Chamber

BA	HR	A	B	C	D	E	F	$\bar{x}$	R
1	1	15.9	15.9	15.9	16.0	16.0	16.1	15.97	0.2
1	2	16.1	16.1	15.8	16.0	15.9	15.9	15.97	0.3
1	3	16.0	15.9	15.8	16.1	16.1	16.2	16.02	0.4
1	4	15.8	15.9	15.8	16.0	16.2	16.1	15.97	0.4
1	5	16.0	15.8	15.9	16.0	15.8	15.9	15.90	0.2
1	6	15.9	16.0	15.8	15.8	16.0	15.8	15.88	0.2
2	7	16.2	16.0	15.9	16.1	16.2	16.0	16.07	0.3
2	8	15.9	16.1	16.2	16.0	15.9	16.1	16.03	0.3
2	9	16.2	15.9	16.0	16.0	16.1	15.9	16.02	0.3
2	10	16.1	16.0	15.9	16.1	16.0	16.1	16.03	0.2
2	11	15.9	16.0	16.2	16.0	15.9	16.0	16.00	0.3
2	12	16.0	15.9	15.9	16.0	16.2	15.9	15.98	0.3
3	13	15.9	16.0	16.0	16.0	15.8	15.8	15.92	0.2
3	14	16.0	16.0	15.8	16.0	15.9	15.8	15.92	0.2
3	15	15.8	15.9	15.8	15.9	16.0	15.9	15.88	0.2
3	16	15.9	15.9	16.0	15.8	16.0	15.8	15.90	0.2
3	17	15.8	16.0	15.8	16.0	16.0	15.9	15.92	0.2
3	18	16.0	15.9	16.0	16.0	15.9	16.0	15.97	0.1
4	19	16.0	15.9	16.1	16.1	16.0	16.1	16.03	0.2
4	20	16.2	16.0	15.9	16.1	16.0	16.1	16.05	0.3
4	21	16.0	15.9	16.1	15.9	16.2	16.0	16.02	0.3
4	22	16.2	16.0	15.8	16.0	15.9	16.1	16.00	0.4
4	23	16.0	16.1	15.9	16.0	16.2	16.0	16.03	0.3
4	24	16.1	16.0	16.2	15.9	15.9	16.2	16.05	0.3
5	25	15.9	16.0	16.1	16.2	16.1	16.0	16.05	0.3

$\sigma_{\bar{x}} = 0.0585 \quad \bar{R} = 0.264$

The correct method of calculating the control limits is based on the same formula as in Section 2.8:

$$\text{Target} \pm 2.33 \; \sigma_{\bar{x}},$$
$$\text{Target} \pm 2.33(0.0585),$$

Target ± 0.136 oz.

As always, careful attention must be exercised when identifying outliers. When the standard deviation is calculated directly (versus from $\bar{R}$), there is always a risk of having the estimate of the standard deviation biased to the high side. From an analysis of Equation 8, one can see that an outlier datum point will have an exponentially biasing effect on the calculation of the standard deviation. From the initial data, anything outside

$$\bar{\bar{x}} \pm 1.645\sigma_{\bar{x}}$$

was considered an outlier, to be temporarily discarded as the average and standard deviation are recalculated. The initial SPC plot, however, will contain all the data, to show the true state of the process.

The $\bar{x}$ chart is shown in Figure 2.27. Note that with every seven observations, starting with hour 7, the common cause batch-to-batch variability often can be seen on the chart. Most of the time, this upstream batch-to-batch variability can be reduced. An expert statistician is needed to help management identify its presence and the fraction of the total variability resulting from this source (components of variance analysis). Then an interdisciplinary team consisting of the statistician, supervisors, process engineers, and operators must work to solve the problem.

For this rotary-fill process, chambers may get clogged such that there is statistically significant within-rotary variability among the six chambers. The R chart of Figure

2.28 can help identify this situation. The$\bar{R}$ and UCL are based on the within-rotary (among chamber) data of Table 2.7.

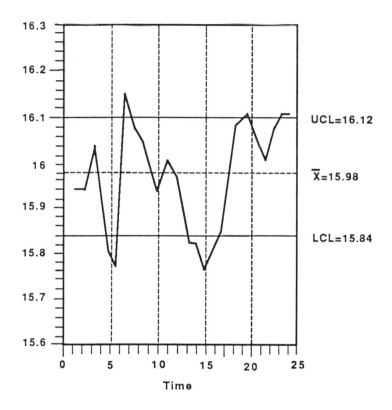

Figure 2.27 X-Bar Chart for Vial Weights

$$UCL_R = D_4\bar{R} = 2.004\,(0.264) = 0.5241$$

When a plotted R point is out-of-control, at least one of the chambers is yielding different vial weights from the others.

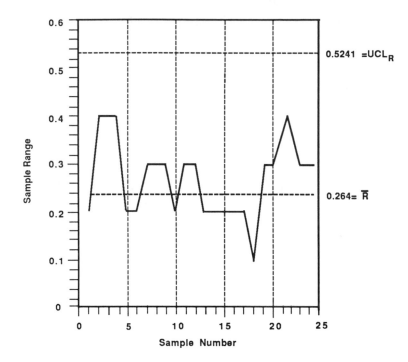

Figure 2.28   R-Chart Showing Within-Rotary (Among
Chamber) Variability

Theoretical note:

If all the individual vial weight data are routinely
entered into a computer where a good statistical software
package exists, the chamber-to-chamber variability may
best be identified in a more sophisticated fashion.
Possibilities may be an analysis of periodicities through an
autocorrelation analysis (either statistical or engineering),

or a Fourier analysis. A more complete, theoretical discussion is provided by Ryan (1989, Section 5.11).[17]

In those cases where one cannot identify which chamber filled a vial, or where the number of chambers is large, the simple procedure discussed previously may be enhanced by considering the section on fill control problems in Montgomery (1985, p. 264).[16]

2.18
Product Variable Changes Over Time

It is common to find unconvinced operators not using SPC charts to control the process, but instead, filling in the charts at the end of their work shift. There are several obvious reasons for this behavior, all the result of improper SPC implementation. One of the reasons is that it is impossible to SPC chart the variable immediately at the output of the product when it changes in-transit to the next department. Consider a product consisting of corrugated flat board that was to be folded and glued into boxes in a subsequent process about 30 minutes later. The board quality variable was a measure of flatness called warp. A board warp of zero was perfectly flat. Management had initiated SPC charts at the corrugator with a target (centerline) of zero. However, there obviously was no resulting improvement in quality.

Upon later analysis, the operators explained that the board warp changed from the up (+) to the down (−) direction over time in-transit to the customer (next department) 30 minutes later. The experienced operators had learned to partially ignore the board immediately leaving the corrugator, and instead to *eyeball* it on the conveyor 30 minutes later just as the customer was about to use it.

It was certain that the process needed to be stabilized through SPC, and it was suspected that the target warp at the corrugator should be greater than zero, since the board changed in the negative direction in-transit. An experiment was conducted where many units of product were sampled every minute from the time of manufacture until used by the customer. The results are shown in Figure 2.29. The new SPC method that was designed involved waiting at least seven minutes before measuring the warp. At this time, they could target at zero. To have an ultimate product average of zero, the board immediately coming off the machine had to have a warp of +4 units, since it changed from +2 to −2 as it dried and stabilized.

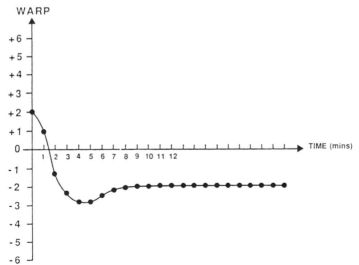

Figure 2.29 Warp Measurements Over Time

This was a simplistic example, but was included to prove a point. In many cases, there are engineering analyses that must be conducted before effective SPC can be initiated. A series of well-planned seminars by a respectable guru often cannot be applied to a present data accumulation system in a turnkey fashion. There usually has to be a designated SPC expert who spends many hours talking to experienced operators and running experiments prior to the installation of SPC.

2.19
Some Special Purpose Charts

Tool Wear

It is possible for a process average to change almost continuously such that one cannot produce to a constant target. The classical case is that of tool wear outlined by Montgomery (1985).[16] As a machine tool wears, the processed part gets larger for outside dimensions, or smaller for inside dimensions. A conventional control chart is of little value in these cases.

One alternative is to establish the slope of the line representing the product dimensional change as the tool wears. The slope of this line is established with simple regression analysis. Then the plus-or-minus control limits can be drawn about the sloped centerline on the control chart. (See Figure 2.30.) As the operator takes measurements and plots points, the chart enables him to ignore expected tool wear and to identify assignable cause when outside the 3σ control limits.

In some cases, the tool wears fairly quickly so that other sources of assignable cause are insignificant between setups, or tool changes, as compared to the tool wear. In these cases, the control chart probably will not be of much use, as compared to the establishment of the optimum interval between tool changes, shown as Δt on Figure 2.30.

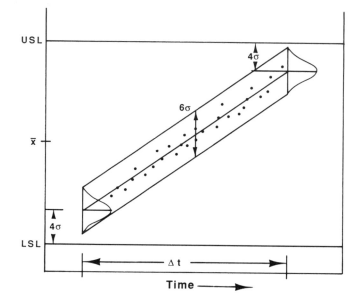

Figure 2.30 Control Chart for Tool Wear

At setup, or tool-change time, pre-control should be used to ensure that the initial process average is at:

$$LSL + 4\sigma$$

Precontrol is discussed in Section 2.10. After time period Δt, the tool is routinely replaced. The useful life of the tool is a function of the slope of the line (rate of tool wear) and the process σ. Note that 4σ is used at both extremes to provide a margin of safety.

In these cases, scientifically establishing Δt , and the discipline of changing the tool on schedule is more important than SPC charting.

Group Control Charts

As discussed in Grant and Leavenworth (1980),[7] it is possible that there are a number of samples from several different sources, and it is desirable to combine all the information on one chart. With a group control chart, only the largest and smallest x̄ are plotted on the chart, rather than maintaining a separate chart for each source. A similar procedure can be followed for an R chart.

These charts may not be good for identifying runs or trends within an individual source. In some cases, however, especially when the sampling interval is wide for economic reasons, identifiable runs or trends may be rare, as compared to assignable cause yielding plotted points outside the control limits. In these cases, group charts may be acceptable as a simplified procedure.

Modified Control Limits

Generally SPC, and thus controlling to target, implies minimum product variability away from some specified nominal. There may be cases, however, where the specification limits are far wider than the control limits and because of economic considerations, the SPC charts are intended as more of a method to stay within specification, versus on-target. In these cases modified control limits are acceptable. The modified limits are set

4σ inside the specification limits. Then, by controlling the process to keep the plotted variable inside these modified limits, at least none of the product will be out of specification. (See Figure 2.31.) The conventional control limits would be 3σ away from target. The modified limits, UCL' and LCL' are farther out at 4σ from the customer's specifications.

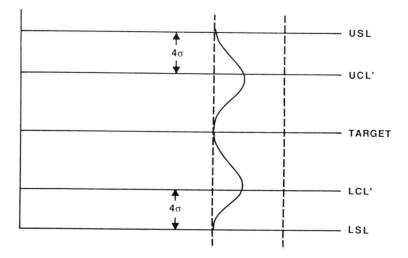

Figure 2.31 Modified Control Limits

2.20
The Future

The thrust of this text is to provide practitioners with tools to be used immediately, so this section on the future will be brief. (For an excellent, detailed [but theoretical] reference, see Keats and Hubele, 1989).[14] As discussed in earlier sections, when the data comprising a sample are not independent uncorrelated specimens, the usual laws of statistics are not valid. The main problem is that when the measure of process common cause is estimated via σ, $\bar{R}$ etc., correlated data will give an underestimated level of process random variability. With some modern sophisticated data collection systems, 100 percent testing is common. Having all the data available can compound this problem of non-independent data. The increasing use of closed-loop automatic control systems also poses some challenges for SPC practitioners, resulting in new ground opportunities. Many instrumentation engineers' understanding and use of control theory is rather deterministic. Hence, with their designs, if any deviation away from target is sensed, a feedback control signal is sent to make an up-front adjustment to the process. Even in the cases where internal tolerances are programmed into the controller, these are often not statistically based. Consequently, periodicities resulting from overcontrol and unstable feedback control systems are not uncommon. These periodicities often are hidden by the randomness in the data, but they can be identified by advanced statistical techniques, see Montgomery (1985).[16]

When a process naturally cycles, some unique challenges arise. The normal methods of SPC do not apply for several reasons. First, there is correlation among consecutive data points. Also, if the periodicity cannot be removed, the spread of the control limits must account for this variability common to the system.

The mathematical tools for these situations are fairly well documented in the literature, but do require an experienced, graduate-degreed statistician, with good computer capabilities. One approach is to use the weighted moving average chart. In other words, each plotted point is the average of the last n points, with the most recent data weighted more heavily. The most commonly used technique is the exponentially weighted moving average (EWMA) where the older data are weighted less according to exponentially decreasingly sized weights. The control limit calculations and interpretation rules are expressed in Hunter (1986).[9] This method overcomes the serial autocorrelation issue among closely spaced data. This technique also can be used as a predictive model to enable the analyst to forecast where the next plotted point may be. For processes with uncontrollable patterns, this predictive capability may be feasible.

Another method by Box and Jenkins (1976)[1] is the autoregressive integrated moving average (ARIMA). This method involves two charts and is especially suited for processes with uncontrollable periodicities. One chart displays the cycling, or periodicities, identified by the computer. Another chart displays the residuals, or random deviations away from the predicted cyclical behavior. These residuals are the common cause. Points out of control on this residuals chart indicate process assignable cause, or deviations away from the norm, thus they warrant investigation.

Another method being investigated for use with automated processes is the Kalman filter model sugested by Kirkendall (1989).[15] This method offers promise over exponential smoothing models for reasons relating to sparse historical data and cases where frequent process interventions are to be made.

2.21
Control Charts for Medians

In most cases it is advisable to have the operator calculate the averages and interpret the control charts if he/she is the one who makes the process adjustments. Chapter 5 outlines the specific training required to enable the operators to perform this function effectively. In some cases, however, it is not feasible to use calculators on the plant floor because of contaminants or security problems. In these cases, control charts for medians can be used. The median of an ordered subgroup is the middle number. Consider the example where an operator is running a machine that dispenses tissue from big rolls of paper from the paper-making process onto small five-inch rolls for consumer use. If the smaller roll diameters are too far from the target, the automatic polypropylene wrapping device will not operate properly. The bulkiness of the tissue on the big rolls varies making it necessary to monitor the process that measures off smaller quantities onto the consumer-sized rolls. A classical $\bar{x}$ chart would work for this process, but the pulp dust was found to contaminate the electronic calculators used to calculate the $\bar{x}$ and range values. The data in Table 2.8 show how median charts were constructed.

Table 2.8 Tissue Roll Diameters

Subgroup Number	Small-Roll Diameters			Median	Range
1	5.1	5.0	4.9	5.0	0.2
2	5.0	5.0	4.8	5.0	0.2
3	5.1	5.0	5.0	5.0	0.1
4	5.0	5.0	5.0	5.0	0.0
5	5.1	5.0	4.9	5.0	0.2
6	5.1	5.0	4.9	5.0	0.2
7	5.0	4.9	4.9	4.9	0.1
8	5.0	4.9	4.8	4.9	0.2
9	4.5	4.2	3.9	4.2	0.6
10	5.1	5.1	5.0	5.1	0.1

$$\bar{x}_m = 4.91 \quad \bar{R} = 0.19$$

It is preferable to use 25 or more subgroups when establishing the median control charts. Ten subgroups were used here for convenience.

The target small-roll diameter is 5.0 inches. The control limits for median charts are calculated as:

$$\text{UCL} = \bar{x}_m + A_m\bar{R},$$
$$\text{LCL} = \bar{x}_m - A_m\bar{R},$$

where the A_m factor is in the Appendix and is based on the subgroup size (n). The $\bar{R}$ is the average range, and $\bar{x}_m$ (or target) is the average of the subgroup medians. The control limits for the ranges are based on $D_3\bar{R}$ and $D_4\bar{R}$ as before. For the above example, the upper control limit for the range equals:

$$D_4\bar{R} = 2.575\ (0.19) = 0.4893,$$

and since the range for subgroup 9 is outside these limits, the 0.6 is discarded and the average range is recalculated as 0.14 unit. The new UCLR = 2.575 (0.14) = 0.3605 unit. It may not be known why, but subgroup 9 does not belong to the same statistical family as the other samples. The $\bar{x}_m$ also is recalculated as 4.99 units.

The control limits for the medians are:

$$UCL_m = \bar{x}_m + A_m\bar{R} = 4.99 + 1.19(0.14) = 5.16 \text{ units}$$
$$LCL_m = \bar{x}_m - A_m\bar{R} = 4.99 - 1.19(0.14) = 4.82 \text{ units}$$

Many firms plot all three measurements on the chart. Then the middle number applies to the UCL_m and LCL_m. A template with the length of $D_4\bar{R}$ can be used on the same chart to indicate if the dispersion is too great to have resulted from chance.

CHAPTER 3
CONTROL CHARTS FOR
ATTRIBUTES

Many quality characteristics can be measured. Examples
include weights, machined dimensions, strengths, etc.
These types of characteristics involve measurements of
variables. The methods of Chapter 2 typically apply for
variables measurements. Other types of quality
characteristics can be observed, but not measured.
Examples of such go/no-go types of quality attributes
include surface appearances, quality of painted finishes,
etc. These types of quality characteristics are called
attributes. Control charts for attributes include p charts
for percent nonconforming, np charts for number
nonconforming, c charts for number of defects, u charts for
number of nonconformities per unit, and charts for
demerits per unit.

Attribute control charts should be used as a last resort
in cases where a variables measurement cannot be
established. Attribute charts are not as sensitive to
process problems as variables charts, and the required
sample sizes are extremely large. If there is a quality
problem, and the main quality variables are attributes,

Section 5.1 on problem solving and the prevention mode probably is the only lasting answer. This is especially true for processes with small, parts-per-million defective levels that must be reduced to zero.

3.1
Control Charts for Percent Nonconforming (p Charts)

Consider a case where an extrusion process is used to make automotive side-body moldings. A variables chart as shown in Chapter 2 would most likely be used for the measurable quality characteristics. An $\bar{x}$ chart would be used for product lengths and modified average charts for product cross-section (see Section 2.11). However, the level of surface blemishes cannot be measured easily. Table 3.1 contains the data from 25 subgroups of 100 items each. These 100 items were chosen randomly over the sampling interval, not consecutively as with control charts for variables. From Table 3.1, there were 120 nonconforming items from 2,500 specimens. A nonconforming unit is one that cannot be shipped to the customer. The average percent nonconforming is calculated as

$$\bar{p} = \frac{120}{2500} = 0.048(4.8\%)$$

The preliminary process average is 4.8 percent nonconforming. Without engineering changes in the process, or formal methods improvements and subsequent operator training, it is extremely unlikely that management can expect fewer nonconformities on the average. You will find that the process average percent nonconforming is largely a function of inherent process capabilities, quantity-oriented employee incentive programs, and management's previous attitudes toward shipping defective product to the customer. These management attitudes probably have remained in the operators' minds.

With a process average of 4.8 percent nonconforming, there will be some chance variability such that some lots will be slightly better or worse. Upper and lower control limits can be calculated as:

$$\bar{p} = \frac{120}{2500} = 0.048(4.8\%)$$

$$UCLP = \bar{p} + 3\sqrt{\frac{\bar{p}(1-\bar{p})}{n}} = 0.1121$$

$$LCL = \bar{p} - 3\sqrt{\frac{\bar{p}(1-\bar{p})}{n}} = 0 \quad \text{(since the value is}$$

negative)

All numbers can be multiplied by 100 to yield percent nonconforming versus the decimal fraction.

With an average percent nonconforming of 4.8 percent, there will be an occasional lot sampled by chance with 11.12 percent nonconforming as indicated from the UCL. The chart is shown in Figure 3.1. Note that sample number 20 is out-of-control. This sample should be

Table 3.1 Number of Defective Side-Body Strips

Subgroup Number	Sample Size (n)	Number of Defectives
1	100	4
2	100	5
3	100	3
4	100	6
5	100	3
6	100	7
7	100	8
8	100	2
9	100	5
10	100	4
11	100	3
12	100	6
13	100	7
14	100	4
15	100	5
16	100	4
17	100	3
18	100	5
19	100	1
20	100	12
21	100	3
22	100	4
23	100	5
24	100	5
25	100	6
	Sum = 2,500	Sum = 120

discarded and the control limits reestablished. In the future, out-of-control points will be circled as the sources of assignable cause are eliminated.

Note in Figure 3.2, the p chart for the same process with a sample size of five. With this small sample size, the odds are that we will find no nonconformities when the process average is 4.8 percent nonconforming. When a nonconforming unit does occur within the sample of five, however, it makes the process appear 20 percent nonconforming; 40 percent when two nonconforming items are in the sample. In any event, as is evident, the p chart looks odd.

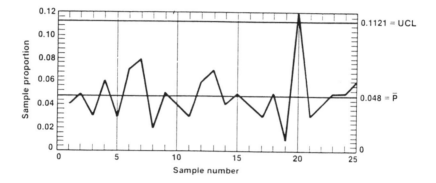

Figure 3.1 p Chart for Percent Nonconforming

As stated earlier, the sample sizes must be large for attribute control charts. For all charts of occurrences of nonconformity, the minimum subgroup size must satisfy

$$n\bar{p} > 3,$$

where $\bar{p}$ is the process average percent defective and n is the sample size. As an example, when the process average is 1 percent ($\bar{p} = 0.01$), it takes a minimum subgroup size of 300 to provide a reliable p chart. For cases of expensive testing, it may not be possible to keep a timely p chart that provides responsive process control information. However, a weekly plot from the last seven days' samplings may give an indication of long-run process trends. If only 50 checks per day are feasible, the 350 total checks for the week may provide a reliable, weekly p chart. With zero percent defect a near-reality and parts-per-million quality levels already having arrived in most industries, one can understand why the prevention mode of Section 5.1 provides the only lasting quality improvement. Interdepartmental teamwork becomes a necessity.

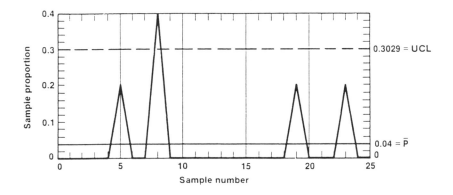

Figure 3.2 p Chart with the Sample Size Too Small

Percent defective charts are useful as temporary investigative tools pertaining to clerical errors, typing, keypunching, etc. Over time, if the process is in control, there is probably a system problem to be designed out by management. (See Section 5.1 on the Interdisciplinary Team.) Local pressure on the clerks will not provide a lasting solution, and will certainly frustrate them. However, an out-of-control chart indicates inconsistencies usually more assignable to the local supervisor or operators.

3.2
Control Charts for Number Nonconforming (np Charts)

In some cases the operators may be uncomfortable with percent defective data. In these cases, the number of actual defectives can be plotted. From Table 3.1, the first number plotted would be 4 since there were four defectives in the first sample of 100 units. These charts are called np charts. The centerline is $n\bar{p}$, or $100(0.048) = 4.8$. The control limits are calculated as:

$$\text{UCL}_{n\text{p}} = n\bar{p} + 3\sqrt{n\bar{p}(1-\bar{p})} = 11.21, \text{ and}$$

$$\text{LCL}_{n\text{p}} = n\bar{p} - 3\sqrt{n\bar{p}(1-\bar{p})} = 0$$

for the initial $\bar{p}$ of 0.048 (4.8 percent) established before the original out-of-control points are discarded. (It is only incidental here that the sample size equals 100.)

3.3
Control Charts for Number of Defects (c Charts)

From the example of Section 3.1, a nonconforming section of side-body molding is one that the customer will not knowingly accept. As an example, for a two-foot length of plastic molding, the customer may not accept it if it contains five or more particles of contaminant under the clear protective surface. Therefore, a defective unit is one that contains five or more particles of contaminant, i.e., five or more defects. A defect is a contaminant particle. A defective unit is one that contains five or more such contaminant particles (defects). In many cases it is more desirable to keep control charts on the number of defects instead of the percent nonconforming. This is especially true when the inherent process capabilities are far better than the customer requirements, but management wants to perform better than is necessary and/or wants to know quickly when the process drifts out-of-control, to enable them to make corrections before the product becomes out of specification. For example, in the side-body illustration of Section 3.1, the process average percent nonconforming $(\bar{p})$ is 4.8 percent. Based on the above definition of a nonconforming unit, this means that on the average 48 out of 1,000 units will have five or more contaminant particles. A p chart for percent nonconforming will indicate if the average percent nonconforming increases, or if the number of units containing five or more particles increases. Assume that the average number of contaminant particles (defects) on a single unit is two when the process is performing within its inherent capabilities, even though 4.8 percent of the time the process creates a nonconforming unit with five or more defects for no explainable reason. Also, assume that the process deteriorates to the point where the average number of defects on a unit is three. A control chart for number of defects will identify this deterioration within two to three plottings. With a p chart, we are unlikely to get a sample with a percent nonconforming above the UCL of 11.21 percent for a considerably longer period of time. Furthermore, having to inspect 100 units for the p chart, versus one item for number of defects chart (c chart), would likely necessitate increasing the sampling interval and losing touch with the process. The data exists in Table 3.2 for a c chart of the side-body automotive molding example. Twenty-five single units were inspected. In each case the number of contaminant particles, or defects, were counted and recorded

The average number of defects recorded in Table 3.2 is calculated as:

$$\bar{c} = \frac{59}{25} = 2.36 \text{ defects}$$

Table 3.2   Defect Data for Automotive Side Moldings

Item	Number of Defects
1	2
2	1
3	0
4	3
5	2
6	3
7	4
8	0
9	2
10	2
11	3
12	3
13	1
14	4
15	3
16	1
17	0
18	3
19	4
20	3
21	3
22	3
23	4
24	3
25	2

Total = 59

Assuming that the process was in a state of statistical control, the typical unit will have 2.36 defects (59/25) or contaminant particles. There will be, however, some chance variability causing some units to have slightly more or fewer defects when the process is in control. The UCL and LCL represent this chance variability and are calculated as:

$$UCL_c = \bar{c} + 3\sqrt{\bar{c}} = 6.9687$$

$$LCL_c = \bar{c} - 3\sqrt{\bar{c}} = 0$$

Here, unless a unit has seven or more defects or there is a run of six items above $\bar{c} = 2.36$, the process will be assumed to be in control. The c chart has been used frequently with painting or coating processes. When points fall above the UCL or there is a run above $\bar{c}$, the process is stopped and the machinery is cleaned or adjusted. Most c charts do not work unless you expect to get at least two or three defects on the average unit. When $\bar{c} < 2$, one can group specimens such that each group has two or more defects. To use a c chart, the group size must remain constant. C charts are useful in clerical situations, similar to p charts.

3.4
Control Charts for Number of Defects per Unit (u Charts)

When $\bar{c} < 2$, or when number of units to be inspected must vary, a defects per unit control chart can be used. The typical subgroup size (n) should be large enough that average or expected number of defects within the sample is greater than or equal to two. The control limits are calculated as:

$$UCL_{\mu,} = \bar{\mu} + 3\frac{\sqrt{\bar{\mu}}}{\sqrt{n}}$$

$$LCL_{\mu,} = \bar{\mu} - 3\frac{\sqrt{\bar{\mu}}}{\sqrt{n}}$$

where $\bar{\mu}$ is the average number of defects per unit, and n is the sample size. Note that the limits vary as the sample size changes.

Consider the example of a lawn mower assembly plant and a process that spray-paints the mower castings. The process inherently creates a small number of paint imperfections, but when sufficient dust and contaminants build up in the sprayer, a larger number of defects occur. At this point, but not before, the process is out-of-control and management should intervene to have the process cleaned up. The data of Table 3.3 were accumulated during a period when the process appeared to be stable. The subgroup size of 10 castings was chosen so that at least three defects would typically be found in a sample. At this point the operator is inspecting approximately 10 random castings every hour. At times, however, castings get misplaced and show up in a later group. So the sample size varies from eight to 12. The average number of defects per unit is calculated as $\bar{\mu} = 69/250 = 0.276$, and the control limits are calculated for sample number 1 as:

$$UCL_\mu = 0.276 + 3 \sqrt{\frac{0.276}{10}} = 0.744(7.44 \text{ for } 10$$

specimens)

$$LCL_\mu = 0.276 - 3 \sqrt{\frac{0.276}{10}} = 0.$$

The limits for sample number 2 are:

$$UCL_\mu = 0.276 + 3 \sqrt{\frac{0.0276}{9}} = .442$$

$$LCL_\mu = 0.276 - 3 \sqrt{\frac{0.0276}{9}} = .110$$

Subgroup number 13 has an average number of defects per unit equalling 1.1 (12/11). Since this is above the upper control limit, subgroup 13 should be discarded and all limits reestablished.

Table 3.3   Number of Paint Imperfections

Subgroup Number	Sample Size	Number of Defects
1	10	4
2	9	3
3	10	3
4	10	2
5	10	0
6	8	1
7	10	2
8	10	3
9	9	3
10	9	2
11	10	4
12	10	3
13	12	11
14	10	4
15	10	3
16	11	3
17	11	3
18	10	2
19	10	1
20	10	3
21	10	1
22	12	1
23	10	3
24	10	2
25	9	2

Total = 69

3.5
Control Charts for Demerits per Unit (D$_U$ Charts)

Some products have too many attributes for all of them to be tracked with separate control charts. Or there may be many observable attributes, none of which is likely to lead to a defective unit, but the combined effect may yield an unacceptable product. The quality of a CRT picture or colored newsprint are two examples. For these situations, control charts for demerits per unit can be useful.

The attributes are typically divided into four classes that carry weights depending on the severity of the defect. Typical classes are outlined below with weights listed.

Critical defects: Weight = 500

Defect probably will affect the safety of the customer or will certainly cause the product to fail when in service.

Major defects: Weight = 100

Defect probably will cause the product to fail or will certainly cause the customer to take corrective action to use the goods.

Minor defects: Weight = 50

The defect may cause a failure in service, but the product will perform its main function. Repeated occurrences will prompt the customer to buy a competing product in the future.

Incidental defects: Weight = 10

The defect will not be noticed by the typical customer as an isolated case. However, several incidental defects in combination will be noticed and will prompt the customer to buy a competing good in the future.

The centerline for the demerits per unit control charts can be calculated as:

$$\bar{D}_u = w_a \bar{P}_a + w_b \bar{P}b + \ldots + w_j \bar{P}_j$$

where the w values are the weights for defective types A through J. The $\bar{p}$ values are the average percent defectives for each defect type. It is typically recommended to temporarily establish $\bar{p}$ charts for each attribute to make sure that the process is in statistical control or stable.

The control limits for $\bar{D}_u$ charts are:

$$\bar{D}_u \pm 3 \sqrt{\frac{c}{n}} \text{ , where}$$

n is the sample size that will be used in the future. The sample size should be sufficiently large such that at least three defects of some class will likely appear. In other words,

$$n\overline{p} > 3$$

should be used to establish the sample size n. The $\overline{p}$ is the average considering all the attributes. The value of c in the formula is calculated as:

$$c = w_a{}^2 \,\overline{p}_a \,(1 - \overline{p}_a) + w_b{}^2 \,\overline{p}_b \,(1 - \overline{p}_b) + \dots$$

As an example from a magazine printing process, Table 3.4 lists the defect types, weights, and p values.

Table 3.4 Magazine Printing Example

	Defect	Weight	$\overline{P}$
A. Sequence:	Order of pages	500	0.001
B. Register:	Relationship of process color dots to each other	100	0.020
C. Color:	Comparison to customer standard	50	0.015
D. Fold:	Position of centerline	50	0.020
E. Trim:	Condition of edges	100	0.050
F. Cross Alignment:	Line up of picture	100	0.010
G. Feathering:	Ink pulling away from dots	50	0.030

The $\bar{p}$ values were based on several hundred quality checks over the last several months. The control chart centerline will be:

$$\bar{D}_u = w_a\,\bar{p}_a + w_b\,\bar{p}_b + \ldots + w_g\,\bar{p}_g$$

$$= 500\,(0.001) + 100\,(0.020) + 50\,(0.015) +$$

$$50\,(0.020) + 100\,(0.050) + 100\,(0.010) +$$

$$50\,(0.030)$$

$$= 11.75$$

The average demerits per unit of 11.75 is a relative number for comparison purposes in the future. The value of c now will be calculated to enable the control limits to be established.

$$c = w_a^2\,\bar{p}_a\,(1-\bar{p}_a) + w_b^2\,\bar{p}_b\,(1-\bar{p}_b) + \ldots$$

$$= (500)2\,(0.001)(1 - 0.001) + (100)2\,(0.02)(0.98) +$$

$$(50)2(0.015)(0.985) + (50)2(0.020)(0.98) +$$

$$(100)2(0.050)(0.95) + (100)2(0.010)(0.99) +$$

$$(50)2(0.030)(0.97)$$

$$c = 1178.44$$

One hundred magazines are routinely inspected per day. By analyzing the p values from Table 3.4, it appears that this should be a sufficient sample size. The control limits are:

$$\overline{D}_u \pm 3 \sqrt{\frac{c}{n}}$$

$$11.75 \pm 3 \sqrt{\frac{1178.44}{100}}$$

$$11.75 \pm 10.3$$

Assume that on a given day there were two type A defects and 10 of type G. The point to be plotted is:

$$\frac{1000 + 500}{100} = 15$$

Fifteen hundred demerits were accumulated over 100 units to yield 15 demerits per unit.

It is important to watch for runs of six or more on the same side of the target when using these charts. With this case, the printing company found that points seldom were plotted outside the control limits unless the product was obviously defective. On many occasions, however, product quality was improved by an identification of runs above the centerline.

CHAPTER 4
Acceptance Sampling and SPC

It can be shown mathematically that if all the relevant processes for a product are in statistical control, there are only two inspection alternatives. Inspect every unit to screen out the defectives, or inspect nothing at all. The decision whether or not to inspect depends on the ratio of per unit inspection cost to the cost of a single defective being shipped to the customer. A break-even percent defective can be calculated as:

$$P_{be} = I/A,$$

where I and A are the per unit inspection cost and failure cost, respectively. If the process average percent defective is worse than P_{be}, every unit must be inspected, otherwise, no inspection is needed. However, you must know the process percent defective and be assured that the process is in a state of statistical control, thus stable, so that the situation does not change frequently away from the process average. The use of SPC is the most reasonable method of maintaining a process in a stable state of statistical control.

In the case of attribute testing, the $\bar{p}$ value from a p chart can be compared to P_{be}. With variables data, establishing the process percent defective is more complex. Referring back to Section 2.7, if the process capability ratio (C_{pk}) is greater than 1.5, the process inherent percent defective can be assumed to be zero. Otherwise, the shaded fractional area of Figure 1.4 must be estimated.

Acceptance sampling involves taking a predeter-mined sample from a lot of a typical size to enable the inspector to decide whether to pass the lot or subject it to 100 percent screening. This technique often is called lot control, whereas SPC involves process control in real time.

Often it is stated that you cannot efficiently inspect quality into a product after the fact; you must set up process control procedures to ensure that the items are made correctly in the beginning. This truism is correct, and SPC has proven to be the most effective method for controlling quality. However, acceptance sampling remains useful for new processes that are in the development phase. If a process is not stable, and thus not predictable, you cannot establish the process average percent defective to be compared to P_{be}. Also, SPC does not work well for a process that is constantly being revised as it breaks down. When trying to use SPC for an unstable process, no sampling interval will seem frequent enough to keep the charts looking reasonable, or the range will be out-of-control more than 20 percent of the time.

In these cases acceptance sampling must be used temporarily until the new process is stabilized. Acceptance sampling provides poor protection for the customer, but it does assure the producer that the lots are not completely defective. The results of a well-managed acceptance sampling plan also provide some feedback to the producer to help him/her establish when the process has stabilized and thus is ready for SPC, especially if the manufacturing manager is held responsible for the total cost of failed lots.

Acceptance sampling plans are based on acceptable producer's and consumer's risks along with an understanding of the level of quality considered acceptable. There are several good references for choosing an acceptance sampling plan.

Acceptance sampling should not be recommended for two reasons. First, it never seems to provide enough consumer protection. Then, when initiated as an interim measure until the process is stabilized, acceptance sampling seems to become permanent. Management lets these plans become the major quality control tool for the future. Many companies cannot understand why they are losing customers when every lot is sampled prior to being shipped. This leads to the second reason why acceptance sampling typically is not recommended. Few managers have the correct understanding of customer's risk or the proper appreciation of the teeth behind acceptance sampling. No acceptance sampling plan can provide even moderate consumer protection in a vacuum. An acceptance sampling plan is no better than the psychological impact that it has on the manufacturing department. When a lot fails, management should not cave in. The manufacturing department should suffer the dire consequences of being held responsible for the screening cost, scrap cost, etc. Many producers do not understand that after-the-fact acceptance sampling should serve as a psychological tool to force the producer to make the product correctly in the beginning.

The present management can be taught and motivated to understand the pitfalls of acceptance sampling. The problem arises when they forget to provide their successors with this training.

CHAPTER 5
Training Needs for SPC

No SPC effort has ever succeeded without thorough training of everyone involved, especially the operators who maintain and respond to the charts. Many firms, however, have either overreacted or trained the operators too early. Either situation can confuse or alienate the operators. The quality control management should be trained first and have a fully developed SPC system before the production operators become involved. You cannot provide a few hours of statistical training and expect production operators to return to the job and seek out applications. Technical management must find the applications and set up the SPC system. Then the operators can be trained and motivated to use a proven system. Don't forget this!

Training needs exist at four levels with most firms: the quality control management, the operational managers, the production operators, and upper management. A typical successful scenario follows.

The training should start with the quality control manager. He/she will be the person to set up the system that makes the largest impact on quality. Consequently, his/her statistical knowledge and appreciation of SPC should be several times that of any other person in the firm. To begin with, he/she should have the equivalent of two college-level statistics courses in which the instructor emphasized hypothesis testing, not probability or decision theory. Next, the quality control manager should attend at least two SPC workshops. The Professional and Technical Development of the American Society for Quality Control (ASQC), among others, conducts good SPC workshops. The quality control manager should have a complete understanding of this book and should have read all the books in the Bibliography. It also is recommended that the quality manager become an ASQC Certified Quality Engineer (CQE).

At this point, the quality control manager should make the decisions about where and how SPC should be used. As special projects, the QC manager or SPC coordinator should oversee or perform the initial sampling and charting before other employees get involved. Some of his/her original assumptions will be proven correct, others will not. With this approach, there will be no selling of mysterious techniques to the other employees.

Many managers have found it necessary to acquire the advice of a statistical consultant at this point to make sure that no mistakes are made. Also, if the quality control manager does not have the time to become a statistical expert, a consultant can make the decisions on the applications of SPC charts. If a consultant is used, it is best to work with a local person who can work on a part-time basis and be available on call. A professor of statistics in a local business school, engineering, or mathematics department is a good choice. However, this person should be an ASQC Certified Quality Engineer (CQE) and should be able to provide a client reference list of firms with whom he/she has worked. ASQC and Ford Motor Company have a list of statistical consultants.

At this point, using company data and examples, the upper managers should be provided visionary SPC training. In other words, what SPC is, how it is implemented, how much it will cost, what the obstacles are, what the payoff is; and most importantly, what management must do to make effective SPC a reality.

The next group of employees to be trained are the operational managers, e.g., department managers, etc. These employees should fully understand Chapter 1 and the relevant parts of Chapters 2 and 3 of this text. All class examples and slides should be from internal process data. The trainer should be able to demonstrate how SPC, if used, would have led to better quality and reduced costs in the past. About three, two-hour sessions should be adequate for this training.

Following the manager's training, the employees should receive two levels of training. First they should receive three one-hour sessions in plotting the charts with many classroom exercises. Then the operators should plot the charts for several days on their jobs. (At this point there are no control limits on the charts.) The operators then should receive the same training given to the managers. After this they should be ready to use SPC. It is advisable to present their immediate supervisor's and upper plant management's testimonials at this point. SPC starts the following day.

Upper management may need some training by one of the top quality control consultants if management has the tendency to do such things as knowingly let defective product be sent to customers. However, pertaining to the technical aspects of SPC, if the quality manager has performed his/her job, it will be evident to top management after several hours of training that SPC should be supported. The quality manager also should have already effectively quantified the quality costs of scrap, rejects, etc., through such graphical media as Pareto or trend charts. Upper management usually deals best with facts and proven procedures, otherwise a quality control manager or temporary visiting consultant will have difficulty persuading them to try SPC to see what happens. Where SPC is needed the most, however, they will be inherently receptive because they are aware of customer returns and decreasing sales.

Often the instructor for all levels of training will be the quality control manager. However, he/she may not be a good choice for several reasons. First, he/she may not have the time. Second, he/she may not have the communications skills. Many SPC efforts have failed because of ineffective trainers. Also, there may be a credibility problem with the quality control manager, especially if upper management has not supported him/her in the past regarding shipping decisions, etc.

Upper management must state emphatically that SPC will be used in all cases found to be beneficial by the QC manager. It cannot be left up to department managers to take the total initiative to make SPC a reality. In a small percentage of my SPC projects I have failed miserably. In every case, it was when weak or uninformed upper managers failed to express their desires. When the desires of management are known, and when there is expert knowledge available, SPC can be implemented efficiently in a typical manufacturing plant over a period of one to two years. A project-by-project approach works best. Do not try to accomplish a plantwide application all at once. The expert (SPC coordinator and/or consultant) will not be able to participate simultaneously in many projects.

I have not yet seen a case where SPC was not worth the effort when it was carried out correctly. After several months, the customers and production operators begin to feel better about the quality of their product. Within a year the process engineers should develop a better understanding of the processes when they learn to distinguish between common cause and local faults. In essence, everybody wins!

The following section on problem solving is a logical follow-up to SPC charting. If you feel you are finished; if you claim, "we have installed SPC," you can bet that it is not working to capacity. When performed properly, the gains from statistical knowledge are so great that it is obvious that we have just begun with the statistical approach.

5.1
Problem Solving

Obstacles

This section contains several tools that can aid in problem solving. However, in many cases it first appears that these ideas are more conceptual models for organizing one's thoughts, than distinct tools such as a micrometer or calculator. There are management teams that solve complex problems effectively with no apparent use of these tools. As one delves deeply into their thought processes, however, it becomes apparent that many of these problem-solving tools are being used informally and under different names. In contrast, some management teams have superb SPC and problem-solving training and could teach seminars in these techniques; however, few long-term chronic problems are getting solved. The day-to-day fires may be extinguished, but there is no vision about to how to prevent the emergencies prior to the crisis stage. There are many obvious reasons behind this lack of vision, e.g., personality issues, not enough technical staff, etc.

However, two not so obvious, but important reasons emerge and will be discussed.

One reason is what I call the *hero-syndrome.* In some organizations, the only way to get noticed among the struggling crowd is to singlehandedly solve a big problem and have this come to the attention of upper management. In other words, upper management has not learned how to promote and reward teamwork, which creates barriers between departments. This behavior was acceptable during the formative years of the firm when there were so many big problems that a person probably could score big on a frequent basis, solving problems that seemed almost tailor-made to his/her particular talents. With the exception of a few of the Silicon Valley type firms, however, most companies have matured technically beyond the days when the problems were so narrow and obvious that sole individuals could make many lasting, significant system changes. Most of today's problems are interdisciplinary and require a team of four to eight varied individuals to identify a lasting solution. The issues today also are seldom short-term, but require many months of investigative and implementation effort.

Upper management must realize this phenomenon and literally force their employees to form interdisciplinary prevention teams to solve chronic problems one at a time. An outline for an interdisciplinary prevention team follows:

    1. Four to eight people with varied skills crossing departmental boundaries.

2. Specialists are called in on an ad hoc basis. The people identified in item 1 are the critical mass and identified by upper management.

3. Team meets 90 minutes per week in a "sacred" place with several walls covered with writing-board space. No pagers, no secretarial interruptions, no calls, etc.

4. Have a kickoff meeting with a meal, testimonials by managers, etc.

5. Team tools are: brainstorming, cause-and-effect diagrams, Pareto charts, flow charts, trend charts, control charts, scatter diagrams, experimental design, common sense, and economic analysis.

6. Meetings in the beginning seem confusing. System problems are confusing and require months (years) to solve. Do not expect to generate a list of action items at every meeting.

7. Do not fall into the trap of reporting at routine business meetings about being on schedule. Often the clock is the problem.

8. There will be theoretical discussions to educate and enlighten that do not lead to

action items. This is the price we must pay for creativity.

9. Have projects result from control charted variables to ensure that system problems do exist. Progress is monitored as you go out-of-control on the good side of $\bar{x}$.

10. Several actions will be required to solve system problems. The team creates an opportunities list with cost estimates, paybacks (or NPVs), priorities, timing, actions needed by upper management, etc.

It is probable that a consultant or a local college professor may be necessary to act as the team coach. The charisma and tolerance for uncertainty may not exist within any of the insiders, not to mention the fact that where this is needed the most, the competition among the members to get all the credit will likely prohibit the team from cooperating with their coworkers. The team should contain at least one communicative nonexempt person. Upper management must state that they are patient and expect a team answer. Management must acknowledge only team solutions.

The second not-so-obvious reason for a lack of vision pertaining to long-term problem prevention relates to upper management's tendency to manage by the numbers with no control charts. Consider Figure 5.1.

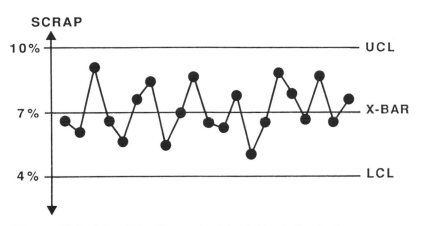

Figure 5.1 Monthly Scrap in Statistical Control

(The limits for this individual's chart are based on the average-moving-range technique of Section 2.9.)

The average scrap rate of 7 percent and the ± 3 percent variability probably are troublesome, but are not a short-term problem that can be addressed in the infamous morning meeting. Since the chart is in statistical control, there are no local faults that the immediate production crew can solve today, or even this month. The situation is chronic in that the team is faced with system problems that probably are interdisciplinary and will require months (years) to solve. The problem(s) is the kind Deming is referring to when he said that 85 to 95 percent of the problems are the responsibility of management. Upper management must organize and train the people to use the concept of the interdisciplinary team. Even more importantly, the local employees cannot be held responsible for a troublesome financial or administrative variable that is mostly in statistical control. If the employees are pressured to do something when only random deviations away from the average exist, ineffective knee-jerk reactions result initially. Eventually, frustration, burnout, and lack of vision (energy) will result. As management stresses quality today, production tomorrow, and waste the next day, etc., the latest issue gets a bandage at the expense of the others. This causes tremendous system variability that makes the problem even worse. For all front office variables used to evaluate or motivate people, there should be a control chart. Upper management also must be able to distinguish system problems from local faults, and to lead the employees through the interdisciplinary team approach for system problems. Now for a discussion of several problem-solving tools. (See Gitlow, 1987;[6] Ishikawa, 1985;[10] and Scherkenbach, 1986 [18] for further details.)

Brainstorming

Under the leadership of a team coach who can tolerate the ambiguity and who has the charisma to get people to talk freely, brainstorming is a valuable technique to generate a creative list of issues, problems, and/or solutions. More extensive coverage of this subject can be found in Scherkenbach (1986).[18] Under typical daily pressures to keep quiet and not look stupid, many creative ideas do not surface. Brainstorming can break this barrier.

The rules are:

1. The problem or issue is explained and then each team member is asked to create a list of every item that comes to mind. Freewheeling

is emphasized. The coach explains to the members that hopefully everyone will have a few wild ideas. They are asked not to critique or evaluate their ideas, just to go with the flow.

2. The coach writes on a big board as each member shares an idea. A member can pass if their list is exhausted. The coach warns that no items are evaluated at this point.

3. The process is repeated until all idea lists are exhausted.

4. The next step is to openly evaluate the list. Some ideas can be combined or deleted.

The list can be incorporated onto a fishbone chart (see Figure 5.2) or left in tabular form. The next step is to prioritize the list based on group consensus. This can take several forms depending on the number of items. In any event the coach is going to summarize the votes in a matrix format during a session. The team members may be assigned a certain number of points to be distributed among the items. Then by combining people's votes in the summary matrix, team members outside 2σ can be given a chance to explain their nonconformance. A new vote can be taken if the nonconformists seem to have a point. Eventually, one to three action items usually emerge. Then team assignments can be made pertaining to investigative or implementation work.

The success of brainstorming sessions is largely based on the coach's finesse. This person must be a good communicator and have no negative preconceived notions formed about him/her by the team members. When this technique works, it can be magic. Usually it is best not to attempt to do all of this during one session. Give the team members time to contemplate the sessions.

Fishbone (Cause and Effect) Charts

Analyze the fishbone chart of Figure 5.2 for a moment.

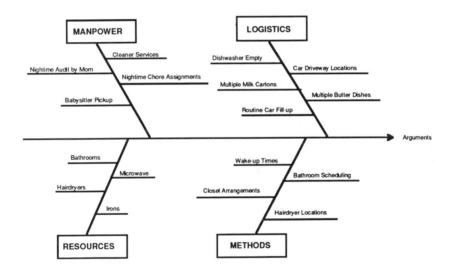

Figure 5.2 Fishbone Chart for Morning Arguments

As a simple example, assume that a family wants to discontinue having arguments in the morning. Through brainstorming the family counselor summarizes their comments on the chart. There is no magic to the chart; it is merely for demonstration purposes. It can, however, make a multifaceted problem appear clearer. Many times in business meetings the group gets into too much detail too quickly. A fishbone chart can help here. The coach can make an emphatic statement that on the first day only the major categories (see the boxes) will be identified. Then on later days each major category will be taken one at a time and discussed thoroughly. A more detailed discussion of fishbone charts can be found in Ishikawa (1985).[10]

Control Charts

The most powerful problem-solving tool is the control chart. A major issue is whether the team is facing a long-term system problem (hence, in statistical control, but bad) or local faults manifested by plotted points out of statistical control. A record-keeping system must be set up so that when a local fault occurs, the assignable cause can be identified and eliminated. Something extraordinary usually leads to local faults. It also is interesting to analyze the periodicities of some local faults.

The situations existing when the charts are in control are usually systemic and will require a detailed team approach. Expect the resolution of system problems to take months or years. Deming (1982)[3] addresses control charts more thoroughly.

Pareto Charts

In the early part of the twentieth century the philosopher Pareto stated that 80 percent of the problems in the world are caused by 20 percent of the people. Pertaining to sociological or manufacturing issues, these odds seem to prevail quite often. It is common for 20 percent of the defect conditions to account for 80 percent of the costs of poor quality. A Pareto chart similar to Figure 5.3 can help managers identify the vital few issues.

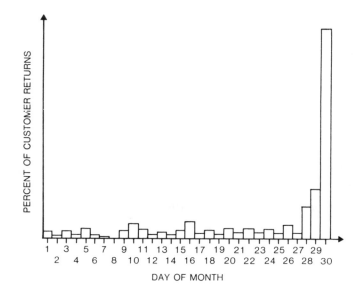

Figure 5.3   Pareto Chart of Customer Returns versus Shipment Date

In this example 80 percent of the customer returns were shipped on the last 20 percent of the days of the month. Obviously, the plant management had a monthly quota to meet so they did anything to get it out the door on time. Ishikawa (1985)[10] gives further treatment of Pareto charts and scatter charts, as well as the trend charts discussed next.

Trend Charts

A trend chart is a control chart with no control limits. This type of chart is particularly useful when only the long-run trend is of interest, or when the average is constantly changing, making a control chart ineffective. Figure 5.4 shows a trend chart for scrap rate resulting from the dismantling of a management by objectives (MBO) system centering around daily production quotas.

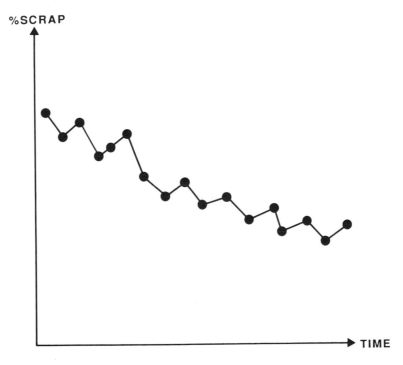

Figure 5.4 Trend Chart for Scrap Rate

Scatter Diagrams

There are many correlated variables in a manufacturing plant. However, common cause (random) variability often makes it difficult to visualize these correlations without a scatter diagram, as shown in Figure 5.5.

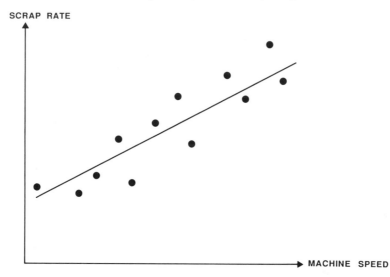

Figure 5.5   Scatter Diagram for Machine Speed versus Scrap

Experimental Design (Factoral Experiments)

A major technical reason making it difficult for manufacturing people to solve problems is the misunderstood concept of interaction among variables. Interaction is the situation where the effect of one variable is a function of the level of another variable. This concept is demonstrated graphically in Figure 5.6.

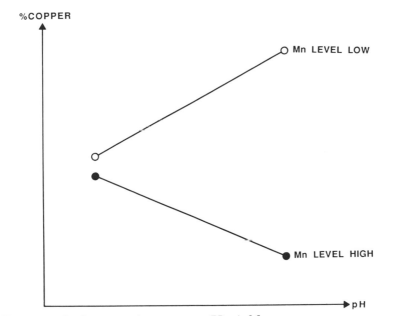

%COPPER

Mn LEVEL LOW

Mn LEVEL HIGH

pH

Figure 5.6 Interaction among Variables

In this case the percent of copper in a brass plating seemed uncontrollable. Upon further analysis, it was discovered that the effect of plating-bath pH could not be identified in isolation. By subplotting incoming steel rod from the the vendors into high and low manganese levels and then running trials with different pH values, they were able to see that as the manganese levels varied, the effect of pH changes varied. In this particular case all interesting levels of each variable were tried at all interesting levels of all other variables. This is called a factorial experiment. Factorial experiments are beyond the scope of this text, but are one of the few methods of identifying interaction. (See Ryan, 1989 for a more complete discussion.)[17] Interaction can be suspected when:

1. Every day seems different.

2. Problems come and go before you can identify the causes.

3. Problems seem different during some seasons of the year.

4. Problems coincide with raw material batch or vendor changes, but not always.

5. Experiments have not been conducted across departmental boundaries.

6. Departments have competing numerical objectives.

To seriously become involved in experimental design, several internal managers must go to a one to three week workshop. The Taguchi or classical approach is acceptable. Then immediately, an experienced professional statistician must guide them through their first several endeavors. Experienced means at the masters level, or above, with several years experience designing industrial experiments. Without some up-front guidance the internal people will become discouraged.

Regression Analysis

We have been discussing factorial designs which typically are used to help establish what the major causative variables of a process are and what the most desirable levels of the variables seem to be. The next level of knowledge that one needs is the functional relationship between the product response variable and the input process variables. As shown, y is the output process response variable and the X's are the input process variables.

$$y = B_0 X_0 + B_1 X_1 + B_2 X_2 + ... + B_7 X_7$$

If one is extremely careful, regression analysis can be used to locate the best-fit functional relationship. However, this typically involves the use of an experienced statistician and a large amount of data. Two or three levels of each variable (X) will not yield a reliable solution unless the relationship is very linear and well defined over the range of interest. A problem with regression analysis and computers is that the best fit equation is always provided, even when this best fit is not a good fit. The computer only locates the coefficients for the functional form specified. If the true functional form has squared terms or interproduct terms $(X_i X_j)$, $i \neq j$, resulting from i/j interactions, unless we know how to specify the functional form, we will get an incorrect linear functional form (by default or intentionally). An experienced statistics practitioner can sometimes spot problems like these.

Many engineers have tried using regression analysis and become frustrated with the obviously wrong answers, such as negative coefficients which are known to be positive. Seven problems with regression are outlined below. One of these probably led to their obviously incorrect answers.

1. The regression computer program only finds the coefficients of the functional form specified. Everything is not linear, and there are an infinite number of nonlinear functional forms that one could test.

2. When gathering data, we often do not have a large enough, or rich enough data set. We need many y values, and corresponding x values. Also, if there is not enough variability in an independent process variable, it will fail to show up as a statistically significant variable.

3. If the instrumentation or process "remembers" from specimen to specimen, or measure to measure, the regression analysis will give wrong answers. Hysteresis, etc., can lead to such problems.

4. The independent variables or the right-hand side of the equation cannot be correlated among themselves. This is an ever-present problem called multicollinearity.

5. The error variance must be constant over the entire range of each x variable.

6. The number of data points must be sufficient to yield enough error degrees of freedom.

7. One or two outliers, or bogus numbers, can greatly bias the results.

There are no intuitive reasons behind these idiosyncrasies of regression analysis. Often, however, an experienced statistician can avoid these problems. Do not be completely discouraged as regression analysis can provide answers to processing issues, but extreme caution is warranted. A special case of regression analysis is the mixture experiment where each X value represents the fraction of a constituent available in the mixture. Thus the sum of the X values equals 1.0.

In many processing-type industries, controlled factorial experiments cannot be run for a multitude of reasons. In these cases, regression analysis of historical data can provide some answers pertaining to the "vital few" variables. Regression, however, requires the help of an experienced statistician. Items 1 through 6 are always prohibitive unless the statistician is streetwise when working with problematic data.

Flow Charts

In some cases flow charts like the one shown in Figure 5.7 can be used during team meetings to clarify confusing process issues.

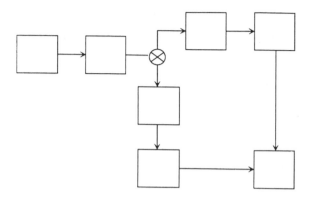

Figure 5.7 Flow Chart

Many experienced interdisciplinary team coaches say that they never delve too deeply into any problem without first flow charting it.

Concluding Remarks on Problem Solving

Many interdisciplinary teams force the discipline of rational problem solving by requiring that all of the aforementioned tools be completed. Usually this is not a requirement, with the exception of the need to always start with brainstorming. Typically it is obvious what the process should be for the team. The important concept is the discipline of forcing the team approach and rewarding team success.

The author has seen many chronic problems solved through the interdisciplinary approach. Some of these problems were in existence for many years as *hero-hopefuls* tried numerous short-termed, patch-up solutions. The team approach is slow, but eventually is successful. The big challenge is for management to encourage team behavior, versus the hero syndrome, and to demonstrate highly visible support and patience.

Appendix
Statistical Constants

Sample Size

n	A_2	D_3	D_4	d_2	A_3	B_3	B_4	A_m
2	1.880	0	3.267	1.128	2.659	0	3.27	1.88
3	1.023	0	2.575	1.693	1.954	0	2.57	1.19
4	.729	0	2.282	2.059	1.628	0	2.27	0.80
5	.577	0	2.114	2.326	1.427	0	2.09	0.69
6	.483	0	2.004	2.534	1.287	0.03	1.97	0.55
7	.419	0.076	1.924	2.704	1.182	0.12	1.88	0.51
8	.373	0.136	1.864	2.847	1.099	0.19	1.82	0.43
9	.337	0.184	1.816	2.970	1.032	0.24	1.76	0.41
10	.308	0.223	1.777	3.078	0.975	0.28	1.72	0.36
11	- -	- -	- -	- -	0.927	0.32	1.68	- -
12	- -	- -	- -	- -	0.886	0.35	1.65	- -
13	- -	- -	- -	- -	0.850	0.38	1.62	- -
14	- -	- -	- -	- -	0.817	0.41	1.59	- -
15	- -	- -	- -	- -	0.789	0.43	1.57	- -
16	- -	- -	- -	- -	0.763	0.45	1.55	- -
17	- -	- -	- -	- -	0.739	0.47	1.53	- -
18	- -	- -	- -	- -	0.718	0.48	1.52	- -
19	- -	- -	- -	- -	0.698	0.50	1.50	- -
20	- -	- -	- -	- -	0.680	0.51	1.49	- -
21	- -	- -	- -	- -	0.663	0.52	1.48	- -
22	- -	- -	- -	- -	0.647	0.53	1.47	- -
23	- -	- -	- -	- -	0.633	0.54	1.46	- -
24	- -	- -	- -	- -	0.619	0.55	1.45	- -
25	- -	- -	- -	- -	0.606	0.56	1.44	- -
26	- -	- -	- -	- -	- -	0.60	1.40	- -
27	- -	- -	- -	- -	- -	0.63	1.37	- -
28	- -	- -	- -	- -	- -	0.66	1.34	- -
29	- -	- -	- -	- -	- -	0.68	1.32	- -
30	- -	- -	- -	- -	- -	0.70	1.30	- -

BIBLIOGRAPHY

1. Box, G. E. P. and G. M. Jenkins. *Time Series Analysis, Forecasting and Control.* San Francisco: Holden Day, 1976.

2. Deming, W. E. *Out of the Crisis.* Cambridge: Massachusetts Institute of Technology, Center for Advanced Studies, 1986.

3. Deming, W. E. *Quality, Productivity, and Competitive Position.* Cambridge: Massachusetts Institute of Technology, Center for Advanced Engineering Studies, 1982.

4. Duncan, A. J. *Quality Control and Industrial Statistics.* Homewood, IL: Richard D. Irwin Inc., 1974.

5. Fellers, G. P. "How to Effectively Use Statistics in a Pseudo-Job Shop." *Quality Engineering,* 2, No. 3, 1990.

6. Gitlow, H. S. and S. J. Gitlow. *The Deming Guide to Quality Control and Competitive Position.* Englewood Cliffs, NJ: Prentice-Hall, 1987.

7. Grant E. L. and R. S. Leavenworth. *Statistical Quality Control,* 5th ed. New York: McGraw-Hill, 1980.

8. Hayes, G. E. and H. G. Romig. *Modern Quality Control.* London: Collier MacMillan Publishers, 1977.

9. Hunter, J. S. "The Exponentially Smoothed Moving Average." *Journal of Quality Technology,* 18, No. 4 (October 1986).

10. Ishikawa, K. *Guide to Quality Control.* Tokyo: Asian Productivity Organization, 1985.

11. Ishikawa, K. *What Is Total Quality Control? The Japanese Way.* Englewood Cliffs, NJ: Prentice-Hall, 1985.

12. Juran, J. M. and F. M. Gryna. *Quality Planning and Analysis.* New York: McGraw-Hill, 1980.

13. Juran, J. M. and F. M. Gryna. *Quality Planning and Analysis: From Product Development Through Usage,* 4th ed. New York: McGraw-Hill, 1970.

14. Keats, J. B. and N. F. Hubele. *Statistical Process Control in Automated Manufacturing.* New York: Marcel Dekker, 1989.

15. Kirkendall, N. J. "The Relationship Between Certain Kalman Filter Models and Exponential Smoothing Models." In *Statistical Process Control in Automated Manufacturing.* J. Bert Keats and Norma F. Hubele, eds. New York: Marcel Dekker, 1989.

16. Montgomery, D. C. *Statistical Quality Control.* New York: John Wiley and Sons, 1985.

17. Ryan, T. P. *Statistical Methods for Quality Improvement.* New York: John Wiley and Sons, 1989.

18. Scherkenbach. W. W. *The Deming Route to Quality and Productivity.* Washington, DC: Ceepress, 1986.

19. Schilling, E. G. *Acceptance Sampling in Quality Control.* New York: Marcel Dekker, 1982.

Index

Individuals, 24, 60
    control charts for, 60
Interaction, 185
Interdisciplinary team, 174

JIT, 78
Job shop, 28, 67

Kalman filter, 139

Local fault, 29
Log-normal, 52
Long-term, 45
Lower control limits
    (LCL), 12, 27

Management by objectives
    (MBO), 183
Medians, control charts
    for, 140
Modified control limits, 135
Multicollinearity, 187
Multiple regression, 188

np charts, 18
    control charts for,151
Natural logs, 53
Natural process limits,
    44, 48
Nonlinear, 188

Operator by-in, 72
Order-to-order, 78, 81
Outliers, 58,65
Overcontrol,
    example of, 9

p charts, 18
    control charts for, 145
Paper machine, 97,100
    CD, 98
    MD, 98
Paper-making machine,
    17,97
Pareto chart,34, 182
Pooled, 66, 101, 105
Precision, 43
Precontrol, 74
Probability distribution, 7
Problem solving, 173
    obstacles, 173
Process performance index
    (PPK), 55
Profound knowledge, 177

Pseudo-job shop, 78

Quality assurance (QA) ,71

Random variation, 5
Range (R), 32
Raw materials,79
Recipes, 68
Regression analysis, 83, 186
Rotary fill, 122
R-square, 186
Rules, 29

Sample size, 28, 43, 75, 148
Scatter diagrams, 184
Serial auto correlation, 57
Shorterm, 45
Sigma, 27, 45, 46
Single-sided specification,
    106
Skew, 73,93
Skewed, 52
Specification limits, 12
    control limits version 12
Standard deviation, 44
State of statistical control, 10
Subgroup, 37
Subgrouping of specimens, 37

Target, 28, 113
Tool wear, 133
Training,
    needs for SPC, 168
Trends, 183
Trend charts,183
t-value, 76

u charts, 18, 156
    control charts for, 157
Undercontrol, 11
Unstable processes, 40
Uppercontrol limits (UCL), 12, 27

Variables data, 16
Variation, concept of chance, 5
Vial weights, 122

Within-order, 58,68